PROBLEMATIC

PROBLEMATIC

How Toxic Callout Culture Is Destroying Feminism

DIANNA E. ANDERSON

Potomac Books | *An imprint of the University of Nebraska Press*

Library of Congress Cataloging-in-Publication Data
Names: Anderson, Dianna E., author.
Title: Problematic: how toxic callout culture is destroying feminism / Dianna E. Anderson.
Description: Lincoln: University of Nebraska Press, [2018]
Identifiers: LCCN 2017050551
        ISBN 9781612349619 (cloth: alk. paper)
        ISBN 9781640120914 (epub)
        ISBN 9781640120921 (mobi)
        ISBN 9781640120938 (web)
Subjects: LCSH: Self-perception in women. | Image (Philosophy) | Feminism. | Popular culture.
Classification: LCC BF697.5.S43 A524 2018 | DDC 305.42—dc23 LC record available at https://lccn.loc.gov/2017050551

Set in Lyon by Mikala R Kolander.

To True and Veebs: the best kids I know.
May you never stop learning and listening.

CONTENTS

ACKNOWLEDGMENTS

This book would not have been possible without encouragement and support from a multitude of people. To those who have stood by me, who have challenged me, who have changed me, I offer my thanks.

To Tom, Natalie, and the team at UNL: you have made such a good home for this book, and this South Dakotan couldn't be prouder.

To Dan, Emily, Rina, Radhika, and Brad: hashtag squad. This book was birthed from many of those late-night arguments as we walked home at 2:00 a.m. and the stories told on Saturday morning brunches over English breakfast. Thank you.

To Dad: I know you don't quite get a lot of what your feminist, liberal, Democrat daughter does, but you've gladly supported me in more ways than I can count. Here's to great homemade salsa and many more years of me teaching you how to Google whether or not something on Facebook is fake.

To my feminist friends and colleagues: here's to being imperfectly great.

INTRODUCTION

In my senior year of college, I discovered Andrew Hudgins's 1987 poem "Piss Christ." I was a theology and philosophy major and was obsessed with the idea of Jesus as a man. I wrote my final paper for my theology coursework on whether or not "sin" was part of human nature and what that meant for a Jesus who was at once fully human and fully God, according to Christian theology. The meaning and power of God-become-flesh—and what it meant to be *flesh*—entranced me.

Hudgins's "Piss Christ" was inspired by artist Andres Serrano's controversial art piece of the same name. The photograph is of a plastic crucifix, complete with martyred Christ, floating in an orangey-red fluid made of cow's blood and Serrano's own urine. Serrano approached the piece as a Christian interested in the utter humanness of the Crucifixion. Christ bled, but he also "shat and peed himself to death."[1] Hudgins's poem reflected on this humanity, commenting that "we have grown used to beauty without horror."[2]

The piece was controversial in its day, and it was still such when I insisted to my theology classmates that we worshipped a Jesus who pooped. It became a refrain of the year, whenever I wanted to knock down someone I saw as being too high and mighty about their friendship with Jesus: "Jesus pooped, too, y'all." I delighted in the "Ugh, but we don't have to talk about it" response that I got.

I convinced myself that I was doing better at this whole theology thing because I had discovered an art piece from the 1980s.

Then again, it was pretty clear that my role at the college was pushing boundaries. When the college was considering cutting its study abroad program, I rabble-roused and organized a series of petitions and letters, mailing them directly to board members (whose names and addresses we students were not supposed to have). I screened R-rated movies in the dorm lounges, which was explicitly forbidden by our dorm rules. I was also the person who, when the college decided to institute a new swearing rule, said quite loudly, "Well that's bullshit."

What I learned during that time was a Christianized version of knowing that art always has something important to say to us as its audience, whether that art is a movie or a poem or a photograph.

It's no surprise, then, that I would bring this same attitude of paying careful attention, challenging the norms, and refusing to be censored into a feminist activist career. Ever since coming into my own in feminism, I have felt incredibly comfortable challenging and changing the ways in which feminist discourse has parsed the meaning of "feminist art." Just as I had been in awe of Andres Serrano's controversial and sacrilegious *Piss Christ*, I was determined to understand and challenge the rubric for determining feminism now.

It took me some while before I became comfortable enough in feminism to trust my own instincts about what was determined to be feminist. I allowed myself to be a student for a time, learning the lingo, and following the drama. Most of all, I learned how to use the word *problematic* in the same way I'd instructed people that Jesus shat in a hole in the ground: with all the condescension I could muster. I'd swung from challenging theology and my native Christianity to challenging feminism through righteous condemnation of anything that was not perfectly feminist.

And I was embraced for it. The more Twitter threads I could do condemning the latest "feminist" beauty campaign or the newly marketed "feminist" TV show, the more audience and platform I gained. The more I could accuse my fellow feminists of failing in their jobs, the better I felt about my own feminism.

But just as shouting about "Piss Christ" didn't actually increase my theological credentials, calling things problematic was lazy thinking that allowed me to focus on a single tree in the midst of a conflagration.

Feminists everywhere have learned how to engage with popular culture on a critical level, but a new cycle has developed that has made it very hard to engage in good faith. Some new piece of art, movie, or fashion trend will come out and everyone will love it for a few days, until that definitive piece of criticism makes us look at it in a different way. Suddenly it's not okay, it's not right, and we can no longer enjoy that thing. And we secret away our defenses and our ideas about things for fear of a feminist backlash, for fear of being the one who causes controversy or, worse, is accused of being complicit in the homophobia, racism, sexism, or ableism displayed by the original piece of work. Our affections, our predilections toward the problematic things, our enjoyment of something in spite of our feminist politics often causes us to behave in secretive ways around those things we enjoy and, on the other hand, to view both ourselves and others as pariahs, as toppled from this inhuman pedestal of perfect feminism once we screw up. The problematic must be acknowledged, must be atoned for, must be issued in a cautionary genuflection lest we be seen as imperfect feminists.

We have made the perfect the enemy of the good.

But this is the pressure feminists are under every day—we can't cover everything, but we feel like we have to in order to understand and be part of the discourse. Admitting when we don't know enough or that we genuinely don't want to participate is often interpreted as a failure of feminism—what are we doing if we are not contributing in some meaningful way to ongoing discussion? We must show ourselves as engaged and useful and interested in every feminist topic and act as guides for other feminists in our engagement with the culture. We're constantly looking around us for signals

We're signaling our feminist virtue with every tweet while binging on *Criminal Minds* and *Girls*. We're accepting of our own secret failures while acting out a life as a perfect feminist by telling fans of "problematic thing *x*" that they're wrong for *liking* something. We don't pause to examine why someone may be drawn to like that thing. We're expecting the performance of feminist values while forgetting our humanity in the process. We call out, clap back, pile on, and win our battles, but we don't pause to think about the wounds we're inflicting or the ways in which we're contributing to a toxic culture of perfectionism.

This book aims to remedy this recent turn in feminist criticism. By applying and connecting modern criticism to existing feminist theory, I hope to navigate you, the reader, through the fraught world of cultural criticism. From One Direction to Nicki Minaj to Jessica Jones to football stars to Lin-Manuel Miranda, I'll examine cultural pariahs and the ways in which feminism has taken them down— sometimes wrongly, sometimes rightly, but always out of a desire for perfection. The standards to which we hold each other create an unreasonable conception of what feminism is and what it means to the larger world—and it's only by going back to basic feminist theory that we can find a way to start this project over, to regain our complicated understanding of what a feminist world looks like.

We are not good at criticism, in the fundamental sense that criticism is supposed to be a push and pull of discussion and discourse. Perfection has become the end-all and be-all of who we are as progressives, as feminists, as people. Our politics have become our identity, and an imperfect implementation of that identity into action is grounds for termination. Art becomes worse when the audience demands perfection of the artist, the audience, and the work.

PROBLEMATIC

1

Lena Dunham Is Not a Pedophile

False Narratives and Scarlet Letters

I have this tweet from 2014 that goes around every so often. It's one of the most popular tweets I've ever made. It's not a joke, an incisive remark, or even a banal observation that caught people's eye. It's a photograph of a page in a book, with a brief description of what's on the page. Every few months, someone picks up the discussion all over again and I watch quietly as my notifications pane fills up over and over with retweets, quotes, and replies about how disgusting the content of this tweet is.

The book page comes from Lena Dunham's memoir, *Not That Kind of Girl*, wherein Dunham makes a joke about "wooing" her younger sister by doing "anything a sexual predator might do." I'd taken the photo because it was what the internet was discussing at the time—casting Dunham as a child predator, as a monster who preys on children. I figured—as with most things online—there needed to be some context, so I went to my local Barnes and Noble and sat in a well-lit window seat to read the chapter. I pulled out my phone and snapped a picture of the page, tweeting it almost automatically. I followed up that tweet with commentary about how I didn't think the joke indicated she was acting with the mindset of a child abuser or that her behavior indicated criminal conduct on the part of the adult Dunham. It was a poorly phrased joke, in extremely poor taste, and one her editors should have cautioned her against including. In full, Dunham was wondering about the concept of uteruses and imagines her younger sister's tiny uterus containing all the eggs she will ever have. Curious, she attempted to look into her sister's vagina and found ... pebbles. Later on, she describes developing an obsession with gaining the affection of her younger sister, writing that "anything a sexual predator might do to woo a small suburban girl, I was trying." But she ends that same paragraph by saying, "What I really wanted, beyond affection, was to feel that she needed me, that she was helpless without her big sister leading her through the world."[1]

Whenever that tweet with the photo of her book goes around, my contextualization of the bad joke gets stripped from the work. And I feel a twinge of guilt because this tweet contributes, in a small way, to the "Lena Dunham, Child Molester" narrative.

This narrative is a strong one, thanks in part to Dunham's own actions complicating her feminist presence long before her book ever came out. Lena Dunham is a young writer, actor, television producer, and director and has garnered an immense amount of fame, and an intense amount of scrutiny, about and because of her work. During her time at Oberlin College, she turned a liberal arts degree into film studies, producing works about sexuality and enlightenment. In one particularly memorable instance, she wore a bikini and filmed herself standing in a large fountain on campus, brushing her teeth. She placed the piece on YouTube, where the comments section soon filled with trollish remarks about her body and her breasts, resulting in her removing the video not long after.[2]

A couple of years later, Dunham's dream of becoming a filmmaker came true when she broke onto the national scene with *Tiny Furniture*, a mumblecore piece about a recent graduate trying to figure out her path in life. The movie was roundly praised by film critics as an accurate, funny, and beautiful portrayal of the malaise of trying to figure out life in your mid-twenties. Lena Dunham was the new It Girl, and that meant a lot to a lot of people because she didn't fit traditional Hollywood beauty standards. Where most starlets were tall, blonde, and thin, Dunham was short, brunette, and chubby—a body described by one commenter as "looking like suet pudding."[3] Her rise to fame as a serious writer, director, and actor gave hope to a lot of people who want diverse body images on screen, not just as the funny sidekick but as an object of sexual desire and a fully realized human being.

Shortly after the success of *Tiny Furniture*, she signed with HBO for the TV show *Girls*, which premiered to great critical acclaim—and great criticism. It won award after award for its first season and was praised by numerous critics as what television needed at the time. Everyone was watching it. Everyone was talking about it. And not everything people were saying was good.

Dunham's media rise and then backlash is a perfect case study for how critique and dismissal work side by side in current feminist discourse. Part of what led to Dunham's downfall was, in fact, Dunham's own claims. She wrote about being a feminist; she proclaimed the label proudly. She campaigned for progressive causes outside of her art world. She wore Planned Parenthood T-shirts on her show and urged people to register to vote. She was a rising media mogul by the age of twenty-four, having produced her own movie and developed a Golden Globe–winning HBO show that brought together feminist ideas with her dark sense of comedy and millennial disillusionment. She claimed feminism, and so set up expectations of what feminist action would look like, and people were, naturally, upset when the image of the perfect feminist and the reality of her actions didn't seem to align.

Girls is, itself, a critique of the very thing it's portraying—mocking millennial problems while also putting faces on them. When Hannah Horvath's parents cut her off financially in the very first episode, Hannah (played by Dunham) responds by telling her parents they're lucky she's not a drug-addicted college dropout. She exhibits immense amounts of ignorance about how the world works while pretending to know a great deal beyond her actual position in the world. She's a college graduate with a humanities degree, convinced she holds some unique dream and unique place in the world and if people would just see her talent, she would have it made.

Hannah Horvath is an asshole. She is White Feminism embodied—which means she considers herself feminist but fails to take a lot of feminist critiques into account, particularly when it comes to issues of race and class. Lena Dunham seems to have purposefully written this character to capture all the good and all the bad: she is self-aware insofar as she understands something of her place in the world, but she is also so self-involved and narcissistic that she thinks she deserves a better place than what she has. In performing this nuanced conception of the narcissistic millennial struggling both with her own lot in life and the social pressure to be a certain kind of person by a certain age, Dunham created a character who critics hailed as the voice of the millennial generation. We were told, over and over in the lead up to and throughout the first season of the show, that this is the show for millennials; this show is for me, and you, and everyone my age. Critic Wesley Morris wrote a reflection in the *New York Times* on *Girls'* fourth season: "When it started, *Girls* was received as an anthem for entitled white women. Detractors had a field day with Ms. Dunham, who created this show and has written and directed much of it, for privileging privilege, as if she couldn't be aspiring to the withering heights of Luis Buñuel or Carrie Fisher."[4]

But as with anything that's marketed and praised as specifically for an entire, diverse generation, the show was not actually representative—because the show is deeply and intensely white. And this was realized with a clapback that reverberated throughout Hollywood and Twitter like thunder echoing off a mountain.

The criticism was encapsulated by an essay from Jenna Wortham at the feminist website The Hairpin, titled "Where (My) Girls At?": "While the show reaches—and succeeds, in many ways—to show female characters that are caricatures, it feels alienating, a party of four engineered to appeal to a very specific subset of the television viewing audience, when the show has the potential to be so much bigger than that. And that is a huge fucking disappointment."[5] Much of the criticism came from a deeply valid place: here is something good, something made by a person who actually seems to know what she's doing, and here, she's failed. Again. Wortham continues: "I see myself and I don't. And I know that the quality of this show means more shows about white people will be made, more shows that don't represent me will hit it big." And that creates a really large tide of programming that is impossible to ignore. "We know better," Wortham says. "We can see that more of the world is like us."

The background of the discussion on representation is as deep as it is tense. Feminism in the United States has racism as a constant background radiation. Because of issues with access, discrimination, and historical failures of inclusion, people of color often must fight to see themselves represented on television. Black women, for ages, have been instructed by white feminists to view the struggles of white women as metaphors for their own lives, even though the struggles are inherently different. Throughout the feminist revolutions in the United States, black women have been placed on the outside. The suffragettes in the 1890s actively fought against the vote for black women. Abolitionism was considered a separate movement from fighting for the right to vote, and many of the leaders of the suffrage movement were not concerned with also fighting for the welfare of freed black slaves. Many suffragettes framed it as an affront that black, property-owning men got the vote before they did, and they fought hard to get the vote without fighting for the same right for black women.

In the mid-twentieth century, while white women were having a feminist awakening about "women's work" in the home, thanks to Betty Friedan's *The Feminine Mystique*, black women were serving as cooks and maids and nannies in many of those same homes. Black women had been "working outside the home" for as long as they'd been in America, and thus the frame of freeing women to have their own careers and lives outside the home didn't speak to the struggle of black women. Indeed, this ongoing tension resulted in a split between a feminism that was concerned with the domestic revolution for white women and a black feminism that was concerned with the issues of property, racism, and freedom of movement that were facing black folk. This latter became known as womanism, as white women had tainted the taste of the word feminism.

This divide continues to form the background for today's discussions about toxicity, about the feminist discourse, and about representation. It is understandable and legitimate that people of color, especially black women, deeply and harshly criticize shows that claim to represent feminist thought. The historical divide in feminist thought demands a careful, nuanced approach to any discussions of representation and of what feminism means for women.

So what happens when a self-proclaimed feminist white woman develops a show, calls it *Girls*, and proceeds to cast all white people in principal roles and people of color in servile positions? It gets noticed and it gets noticed quickly. Dunham's nepotism in hiring for the show (almost all the principal actors are her friends or the daughters of people her parents are friends with) and her missteps in defending the show as reflecting a self-segregated New York City that is still New York only added fuel to the fire. The criticisms were largely right—the representation of people of color on the show in the first season was abysmal, and the show itself was navel-gazing, hipster-y ridiculousness—aka white nonsense. Many of the antics on the show were the result of naïve whiteness and white privilege—do you think a black woman could accidentally take crack and go running naked through the city without some kind of run-in with law enforcement, as Shoshannah does in the very first season?

There are two separate and competing narratives about feminist criticism which, while not originating in the *Girls* controversy, are particularly salient in this case. The first is the idea that any criticism of feminist work must be done in specific—meaning nice, kind, and subservient—ways to be heard. The second is the idea that a person who claims the label of feminist must therefore be subject to a standard of ideological purity that allows dismissal from the club with any infraction on a version of feminism, to be determined by the critic. Both narratives—the tone policing from those who are being critiqued and the tendency toward ideological purity on the part of the critics—swirl together to create a monster of narrative that makes discourse impossible, that makes people fearful of speaking up, and makes it very hard to create or produce any kind of popular culture with feminist elements.

The ways in which Dunham's media team and writers responded didn't help to engage critically. Instead, Lesley Arfin, one of the writers on the show, tweeted a joke: "That thing that bothered me about Precious was that it wasn't about ME."[6] Arfin's joke, meant to highlight the idea that not all stories are for all people, instead mocked the critics and seemed to characterize their valid concerns as whining. The derision present in Arfin's tweet invited derision in response—and from there the discussion became an angry backlash, which segued into an ongoing, contentious battle about the supposed "toxicity" of Black Twitter and Famous White Feminists. The battles did not start with *Girls*, but *Girls* brought them to the mainstream.

In the social media landscape, Twitter reigns supreme as a feminist outlet. Feminist scholars and activists organize, discuss, and promote various ideas and their impact on the overall discourse. It is, largely, where discourse is happening. But like any social arena, feminist Twitter has found itself divided into multiple factions. There's "hammer and sickle" Twitter (socialist activists), Anon Twitter (anarchists, mostly), Black Twitter (composed mostly of black people having their own discussions), Trans-Exclusionary Radical Feminism Twitter, and White Feminist Twitter. This is only a sample, but frequently Black Twitter and White Feminist Twitter find themselves at odds, with Black Twitter using the means at their disposal to critique and demand change from White Feminist Twitter.

The narrative that Black Twitter is a toxic space of criticism developed staying power—handwringing essays about the toxicity of the internet, using mostly examples from black women writing on Twitter in very specific contexts, began to proliferate. Like clockwork, every few months some white person publishes an essay about the toxicity of online spaces and the increasing impossibility of reasonable discussion. Inevitably, the examples are pulled from uncharitable readings of tweets from black women—often the same few black women who are the uncredited sources behind a lot of op-eds and aggregated stories. Their tweets are pulled by BuzzFeed, Mic, TIME.com, and other high-profile news organizations without consent or even notification, only to open them up to further harassment by sharing their words with a much wider audience. Then, after months and possibly years of harassment because of this unwanted higher profile, these same black women get the joy of being used as examples of toxicity in the discussion—often because they weren't "kind" (read: servile) enough toward someone who was berating them over a tweet that got quoted in BuzzFeed. White people are assumed to have the best of intentions at all times, even when demanding a free education about an issue from people of color. People of color are cast as ungrateful, toxic, and, yes, problematic when they dare refuse such demands upon their time and their energy.

Criticism is a hard thing to get right, even among people who are sociopolitical equals. Telling my white friend who attends the same prestigious graduate school that I do that he's fucking up in his commentary about race and speech is an incredibly delicate maneuver—not just because it's hard to find the right things to say in the moment, but because we're human and cannot erase that humanity to become performers of flawless feminism. It's hard to tell someone they fucked up, and it's harder still to realize that *you* fucked up. Add in the intersections of race, class, sexuality, gender, and various forms of privilege and you have a recipe for disaster. Miscommunications, poor responses, and hundreds of years of oppressive relationships come to bear on the discussion, making it virtually impossible for the discussion to remain productive.

More often than not, the result of a critique from a black woman toward a white one results in whining, tears, and ardent defenses about how "not racist" the white person is. And the critics are cast as mean girls purposefully destroying the life and reputation of a well-intentioned white woman. The dispute plays itself out over and over: white women are well-meaning. Black critics are malicious.

Typically, this tension is brought to bear using the only tools many of us have available (social media, online articles). The public nature of such discourse ends up muddying the waters in a lot of ways, making it possible for the low-hanging fruit of simple declarations to be spread quickly and widely. The discussion, rather than being about questions of representation and self-segregation, becomes a yelling match about how Lena Dunham is or is not definitively a racist.

And the narratives proliferate. Lena Dunham is racist. Lena Dunham is a child molester. Lena Dunham is Islamophobic. Lena Dunham is not worth listening to, ever again. She's failed too many times. Her comments are not worthy of patient correction or discussion anymore; she is a disgusting bitch, a dried up cunt, a racist old hag.

All those insults in the sentence above are things that have appeared in my Twitter mentions as the result of that one photo I tweeted two years ago. They aren't directed at me—they're all directed at Dunham. Sometimes the person will tag Dunham in the tweet, just to increase the possibility of her seeing it. And every time one of those appears, I hope to God she doesn't see it, that she has managed to tune out the harassment that her dismissal from the feminist sphere has enabled—the harassment coming from people who want to prove themselves better than she is, so they rail on her reputation with misogynistic insults and slurs.

Such harassment is largely unchecked and unseen, thanks to large systemic issues with the way online harassment operates, but also with the way which once-iconic feminists are swept aside due to an inability to handle controversy perfectly. None of the controversy surrounding Dunham is manufactured—it has, at its root, very real critiques about the necessity of intersectionality and the importance of diversity within social circles. Dunham's work does, in fact, suffer from a malady of privilege—white privilege, straight privilege, cisgender privilege, class privilege. And Dunham's perceived mishandling of that privilege quickly becomes yet more evidence of her failure as a human being.

The "Dunham as child molester" narrative is one particularly harsh example of how quickly the imprecation of a person's ideas becomes conflated with the person themselves. Much of the blowback for Dunham's tone-deaf jokes about her relationship with her sister came—and continues to come—from a place both of misunderstanding and willful mishandling of the facts. Dunham's stories about her relationship were wrenched from context and positioned in the most unfavorable light possible. Her sister herself has said that the charges that she was abused by her older sister are ridiculous. Dunham's stories reveal a person who was not taught properly about boundaries, who did not—as a child—understand that other people's bodies do not belong to her. They do not, however, reveal the malicious forethought and intent of a predatory pedophile who specializes in hurting little girls, which is how they have been characterized by the media firestorm created by her comments—a firestorm, it must be noted, started by an op-ed on the conservative political wonk site Truth Revolt.[7] Such narratives do immense harm both to Dunham and to childhood sexual abuse victims. They also perpetuate narratives about childhood sexual abuse that blur the line between fairly normal exploration and outright abusive intent.

Let me explain. For two years in my late twenties, I worked at a local day care center to help supplement my freelance writing income. I worked with every age, from infants to children up to six years old, but I worked most frequently with the older, pre-K–aged kids. These kids were intelligent, quick, and immensely curious about the world. This also meant they were immensely curious about their bodies and the bodies of other people. Once, when holding a three-year-old, he became curious about my breasts and pulled down my tank top to look at them, resulting in me accidentally flashing a playground full of kids for a few seconds. At other times, kids came out from the bathroom without their pants on, either from some previously unexpressed motivation to Live Free that day or from having had an accident and not wanting to tell the teachers. Seeing other naked kids is just kind of a fact of life when they're that young. It happens, and none of it is inherently sexual in nature.

This curiosity, too, can lead to behavior that is immensely strange to adult eyes and has to be curbed. We had one three-and-a-half-year-old who was intensely curious about butts—her own, other people's, statue butts, dog butts, boy butts, girl butts, any kind of butts. She was the Tina Belcher of three-year-olds. And she pursued her curiosity with the relentlessness of Alice chasing the white rabbit—for a time, we had to talk with her every couple of days about how she cannot pull down other kids' trousers and that other kids don't like it when she does that. She played this game with kids of all ages, and it became kind of an exchange market common to kids: "I'll show you mine if you show me yours." We teachers put a stop to it immediately and told the parents and put in safeguards to prevent this behavior in the future. It wasn't a situation that rose to the level of mandated reporting—it was just kids being kids, and we helped them with setting boundaries and establishing ownership over their own bodies and learning that other people's bodies are not toys for them to play with. Kids are genuinely weird, but a careful eye can spot the difference between malicious abuse and exploration.

Dunham's actions fall into "weird kid behavior." Those accusing Dunham of being a child molester, appending the phrase to her name whenever she comes up, are taking honest recollections of childhood incidents, told poorly, and stretching them to cast Dunham as a monster. In the process, they undermine potential understanding of how predators work and ignore the testimony of

Dunham's own sister, eliminating her agency and voice. The narrative allows for the dismissal of an already disliked person based on quite specious ideas and a lack of evidence. It's a trial by fire, in which the judge, jury, and executioner have been sharpening their axes for years, waiting for their chance.

Likewise, it is fear of this kind of treatment that has burrowed its way into the feminist psyche. I once had the opportunity to see feminist author Naomi Wolf speak on a panel about abortion and the language that pro-choice activists use. The panel was arranged to discuss the impact of feminist dehumanization of fetuses during discussions of abortion and reproductive politics. The entire premise was deeply compelling: are feminists guilty of alienation because we dehumanize what is, to many, a very real and very important part of their experience of their own bodies?

But rather than developing the topic at hand, the discussion became about Wolf's own paranoia, which was on full display for everyone to see. Wolf took what was seen by many in the room as a traditionally pro-life stance, which surprised the audience. She argued that men need to be included in the debate, that feminists need to develop a "seamless web" of consistent ethical behavior around abortion, and that we need to do a better job of giving options other than abortion—all of which are arguments traditionally stemming from anti-choice rhetoric. But when other panelists attempted to summarize her argument and respond, Wolf would interrupt, saying, "That's not what I said!" At one point, with voice raised, she became visibly upset at the very thought that her fellow panelists were taking her out of context, when it was clear to the audience that the panelists were simply trying to understand and rephrase her argument in a clearer way. But she was having none of it—she would be quoted and correctly understood, and she would not be misconstrued in any way, shape, or form. She would be understood or she would walk out.

Wolf's paranoia about how her words could be twisted was not the result of some weird feminist going off the deep end. Rather, it was a somewhat reasonable response to having lived one's professional life under an intensely critical microscope. Her book *Vagina* had received heavy criticism from the feminist world, in ways that I'm sure she felt had manipulated and changed her words and her ideas. To have one's ideas rejected so vociferously and one's own words misused against you must create a level of fear about ever saying something in public again. Humans aren't built to live under the scrutiny that modern critical culture puts on them, and Wolf's erratic and vehement responses in that panel seem to be the result of enduring years and years of such scrutiny without a safety net.

I imagine Dunham's account of her childhood behavior toward her little sister, as someone who felt distanced from said sister and who has struggled with family relationships, was a hard story to write. Memoirs are not easy. Book publishing is not easy. And it's even harder when people are expecting you to fail. And it possibly becomes even worse when a poorly thought-out joke becomes the scarlet letter you must endure any time you want to do your job or to add something new to the feminist discourse.

All of us have these scarlet letters emblazoned across our chests whenever we enter into discussions. For many in the Christian realm, I am the Fornicator, the Feminist Who Encourages Bisexuality and Premarital Sex. I am Angry and Stubborn and Annoying. I'm a massive asshole. (I mean, that last is probably true: I once spent an entire month purposefully trolling Christian blogger Matt Walsh in an attempt to get him to block me on Twitter).

I'm also a human being who's trying to figure out how to pay off her student loans while also working to make the world a better place. I'm making choices that might be different from yours, and I'm doing what I can to live up to the title of Feminist. I can't get rid of how people perceive me and I can't change the people who don't want me in the discourse (and I also know that there are discussions I'm not entitled to be part of). But like many who claim the title of Feminist, along with the attendant complications and discussions and ongoing consternation, I know that we can only move forward with the recognition of both our shared humanity and the ways in which the social constructs around our humanity have shaped both oppression and justice.

The scarlet letters that current discourse has slapped upon people deemed "problematic," deemed "unreachable" for feminism, have created consternation, paranoia, and fear in feminism. Callouts can happen. We need to call out people who are failing to account. We need to have "come to Jesus" talks. But I'm increasingly less convinced that pinning each person who messes up with an asterisk after their name, disavowing them for whatever problematic thing they've done in the past, is necessarily the way to go. If hypercritical feminism is finding its circle of influence shrinking, perhaps it's time to look inward and figure out exactly how and where we've gone wrong. Perhaps it is time to think deeply about our methods and our actions and the humanity of those we encounter.

2

Harry Styles Is (Probably) Not a Creep

What Makes You Beautiful and the Male Gaze

When I was twelve years old, I somehow convinced my father to drive three hours on a Sunday night to go to an 'N Sync concert. We had "limited view seating," which meant we couldn't see the entire stage, but it also meant we were closer to the stage than 80 percent of the audience and could actually see a little bit of the backstage area as well.

Twelve-year-old me was *thrilled*. It was a loud concert, full of screaming girls and even louder music. The men—because by that point, they were grown men—sang and danced and encouraged the audience to scream louder and harder. The dancing and songs were squeaky-clean, hinting at sexuality without actually diving into sexual topics and questions. This, after all, is how boy bands have to be: clean enough that parents don't start boycotting them, and just over the line enough that the older teen fans can see something of worth in listening to them.

The exchange between band and audience is no doubt a sexualized one—each one giving the other an energy that goes beyond the stage and into fantasy. The concert experience, for twelve-year-old me, could arguably have been my first understanding of what it means to hold someone's gaze and to be enraptured by them. Manufactured and calculated, to be sure, but orgasmic and creative and unencumbered at the same time. It was twelve-year-old me's first encounter with the power of popular music, but definitely not the last.

A decade later, when the British boy band One Direction burst onto the scene, it was a calculated and business-savvy move by their record label. They'd been brought together by record label mogul Simon Cowell on the British TV show *The X Factor* and turned into a boy band: a slick, painstakingly fashionable, straight-from-the-factory boy band. Their first single, "What Makes You Beautiful," has been referred to as "the male gaze in a song" and "anti-feminist" by numerous critics, and has resulted in their dismissal from serious music throughout their career. The song's cheesy lyrics with the accompanying squeaky-clean music video made most reasonable adults roll their eyes, and most reasonable feminists worry about the lessons this band was teaching to young girls.

Initially, everything about One Direction screamed douchebags.

A major reason that they were attacked and dismissed so vociferously and so quickly was that they were young men catering to young women. The popular feminist blog *Feministing* published an article titled "One Direction to Girls Everywhere: Your Low Self Esteem Is Hot." A writer for Thought Catalog wrote that the song implies a "logic that a young girl's beauty lies in the male gaze by which she's perceived."[1] The "male gaze" comes up over and over again in discussions about this particular boy band, though it's certainly not unique to them. But it's been misused and abused by feminists just barely familiar enough with the theory to use it as a lens for critique, but not familiar enough to understand its context.

In feminist criticism, the male gaze has become shorthand for a psychoanalytic theory of film spectatorship developed by Professor Laura Mulvey in 1973 in a landmark essay entitled "Visual Pleasure and Narrative Cinema." In this essay, Mulvey proposes that film-making and the design of a film and the narrative of a story is developed in a manner to cater to men who are watching and who want to identify with and objectify the female-identified characters on the screen. Essentially, cinema and entertainment are built so that men may look at women. Women are socialized to be the object of the male gaze, while the man gazes and controls. The experience of cinematic art, Mulvey writes, is developed to cater to a man's pursuit of women as objects, as playthings, as sexualized toys.

The academic conversation surrounding Mulvey's essay has been a wide-ranging discussion, with filmmakers and artists themselves becoming aware of the presence of the male gaze and actively working to counteract its effects. Simultaneously, as this conversation between academics and artists happened within the film industry, the concept of the "gaze" widened out further in popular feminist discourse. People realized that the "woman as object" aspect of the gaze could be easily applied to other axes of oppression: the "White Colonial Gaze," the "Straight Gaze," the "Abled Gaze."

Critiques of the gaze have risen alongside its popularity. Craig Saper, writing in the journal *diacritics* in the pre-internet time of 1991, commented: "To preserve the transcendence of interpretation, the gaze became associated with the function of the eyes rather than anything which might disrupt vision. This situation explains why apparatus theories and the more recent manipulations have difficulty in understanding the gaze in terms other than confrontation."[2]

In other words, because current models of gaze theory assume a strict binary of men looking at women, the theory is inadequate for explaining all the different viewership experiences that happen within cinema—the fact that an audience watching a film is *not* solely male. Saper goes on to argue that "the gaze . . . unsettles empiricism and sets in motion the (re)appearance of gaps, fadings, and flickerings in our perception and understanding."[3] Discussing and recognizing the gaze creates a strange awareness of one's own critical lens and viewership, making it hard to delineate between the outgoing gaze and incoming entertainment. We are too aware of our experience as audience.

Additionally, in dissecting feminist film critic Mary Ann Doane's accountings of the gaze, scholar Jennifer Hammett argues in *Cinema*

Journal (the journal of the Society for Cinema and Media Studies) that feminist film critics are in a bind—they must both account for the effect of the patriarchal gaze upon their own viewing and attempt to enact an "alienation" from that embodied experience. We must at once be aware of the experience of being gazed upon and wrench ourselves free of that experience in order to analyze it. Hammett writes: "Doane's account of the 'psychical force' of patriarchal representations leaves open the possibility of another spectator/text relationship: it is possible for the spectator to resist the seductive power of the patriarchal representations, as long as she remains alert."[4]

Within the discourse surrounding how we receive and react to media, we exist within a paradoxical realm. "The spectator is always in discourse, always the subject of beliefs," Hammett writes. While Hammett is writing about the larger, academic problems present within the idea of the "objective feminist critic," she's hit upon a problem inherent within gaze theory—namely that we are both watching and responding to the gaze and not fully active nor fully passive in our consumption of entertainment, particularly if such entertainment is a live performance.

Mulvey's essay referred specifically to the cinematic experience, which at the time of her writing was exclusively a commercial and social enterprise—there was no "Netflix and Chill," no rental stores, no pay-per-view, no Amazon Fire TV Stick. Movie theaters were centers of experience, playing a role in civil life that has become increasingly fractious. The invention of VCRs and then DVDs and now online streaming make it much harder to draw straightforward conclusions about the audience and the nature of the movie-viewing experience (Mulvey herself acknowledges this change in viewing experience in her editorial introduction to the 2015 essay collection *Feminisms*).

The broadening out of gaze theory has, in many ways, been beneficial. It gives feminists a lot of interchanging lenses for understanding and interpreting the entertainment around us. "The male gaze" has become shorthand for discussing how women are represented on our various screens as objects for male titillation. But this divorcing of an academic term from its specific academic context has led our criticism into a neutered version of the male gaze, separated from its psychoanalytic roots and from the theories of spectatorship in which it resides. By leaving the world of theory behind, we end up either applying the term inaccurately or overusing it to the point of meaninglessness. Our engagement with the term turns it into an invective, an argument ending point, rather than a theoretical exploration of the dynamic between artist and audience. This is what happens when feminist critics dismiss boy bands or directors or artists as having "the male gaze." It is meant to insult and curb further discussion—it is the declaration of "problematic."

The response to the 2015 movie *Ex Machina* demonstrates how the shorthanding of "gaze" neuters what could be a fruitful argument. In a closely bottled, tightly shot film that is confined to one area of the world and that area only, we have three main characters: Nathan, Caleb, and Ava. Nathan is the genius robot creator—he built Ava. Caleb is an employee at Nathan's company who is chosen for a special week's retreat at Nathan's house, for reasons unknown to him. When he arrives at the slick, modern, Japanese-styled estate in the middle of the mountains in Norway, Caleb is informed that he will be playing the human role in a weeklong Turing test of Ava. The Turing test is a test of artificial intelligence, in which a human being interacts with a computer and attempts to determine if they are speaking with a computer or a human based on the responses. True artificial intelligence mirrors human thought in ways a computer is not supposed to be able to predict.

Many critics, including feminist critics at *Bitch* and *Feministing*, took the work to be a classic example of science fiction using female bodies for the projection of male fantasies—in other words, a textbook example of the male gaze. The director, Alex Garland, they posited, did not do his due diligence in subverting or responding to the sci-fi tropes upon which *Ex Machina* rests. As a result, numerous feminists have dismissed the film, including an expert tutor of mine.

But this critique is a misinterpretation of the film. It dismisses too quickly what conversation the director is engaging and ignores the manipulation of the male gaze as a benefit to the storyline. Using the "male gaze" as shorthand for quality feminist criticism is lazy. The discourse around *Ex Machina*—or rather, the lack of disagreement about its interpretation—demonstrates this lazy application of the male gaze into criticism perfectly.

Garland is engaging with contemporary criticism of gaze theory—arguing that it fails to capture the reality that men *and* women (and queer people of all genders!) are watching and absorbing cinema at the same time, which complicates the idea that cinema as an art is built mainly for male consumption. Feminist theory argues that we live in a world wholly dedicated to the objectification of the female body, but male gaze theory, as put forward by Mulvey, is focused explicitly on entertainment, not everyday life. Male gaze theory discusses how a specific mechanism of entertainment is built by and for the patriarchy; to extend the theory out to the real natural world is to go beyond the bounds of the theoretical approach. "Male gaze" refers to the cinematic experience of a man (the subject) looking at a woman (the object) and creating her in his image. In a way, critics are right about *Ex Machina*: it *is* the product of a male gaze.

But *Ex Machina* develops a conversation—previously untouched by gaze theory—in which the audience is both gazer and the gazed-upon. The robot character of Ava is the product of the male gaze—she is created for sexual stimulation on the part of Nathan, her abusive inventor. But it's far more complex than that, because she is artificially intelligent, an inventive thinker. The entirety of the plot twist of the movie rests on the audience—even women—buying into the male gaze theory of how she functions: that she exists for men. The horror in how we respond to Ava's eventual escape from Nathan and Caleb is built out of the audience buying into the consumption of her as an object.

Throughout Garland's work, Ava develops a sense of self and understanding of her own gaze that responds to the false production of her selfhood developed by the male creator's lens. Her being-in-earth owes its existence to the lascivious gaze of her genius male creator, but her power as a woman lies in her ability to return that gaze, unblinking, unflinching, even at the last moments of her creator's life. This is the twist: the object returns the gaze, responds autonomously, and *kills her captor*, the man whose gaze brought her into being.

From the start, Ava and Caleb are positioned to maximize the influence of their gazes on the audience. But Garland performs this in an unexpected way. Caleb is there to observe Ava, but he does so from an enclosed glass box that juts into Ava's living quarters. He is unable to reach her or move around much, while she can disappear and reappear and show herself to him at will. He is forever seen, while she may choose to be unseen. The unsettling nature of this is the result of the gaze being flipped on its head—Ava slowly and surely moved from the position of gazed-upon to gazer, returning his consumptive male gaze with a stern, feminine one. His gaze wants to consume her through "rescuing" her from her prison. But her gaze says, "You are my prison guard and you don't even realize you've imprisoned yourself in the process."

Garland's manipulation of the variant gazes throughout his work brings the power of the feminine gaze into the conversation. It's necessary to realize that the feminine gaze is empowered to return the gaze of the male, and that a male gaze, while dominant, does not land on passive objects or passive receivers. It is controlling, yes, and permeates much of how women present themselves in modern culture, yes. But it can also be returned unflinchingly and become part of a dialogue. Incorporating the returned female gaze into how we discuss objectification is an important part of understanding the developing world of popular culture criticism. *Ex Machina* demonstrates the active engagement of the feminine as a response to the male gaze—engagement to the point of overcoming and killing off that which objectifies. That final moment of Nathan's life, when Ava forces him to stare at her while she kills him, is the feminine responding to the attempted consumption of her life as a feminine object. It is the returned glare of millions of sexualized, objectified women.

Feminist critics miss this introduction of the active feminine gaze far too often.

And this brings us back around to four English, and one Irish, boys singing harmony over a manufactured beat. The criticism of such work—of boy bands, of pop music—assumes the existence of a singular, unidirectional male gaze, of men gazing toward women and objectifying them. The songs point to women as objects, critics argue, creating a world that teaches young women that they are objects created for men. But One Direction, as an entity existing in the real world, also experiences a peculiar, intense female gaze that positions the band members as objects for sexual consumption. While "What Makes You Beautiful" appears to be about how women don't know themselves until a man gazes upon them, it is also about invoking a fantasy in which a handsome man is captivated by a woman. While it is about buying into and selling a fantasy of male attention, it is also about a fantasy of male sexual availability, which is far more complicated than just a male gaze landing upon a passive woman.

Boy bands, in particular, depend on a complex relationship between the male and the female gaze, between the heterosexual consumption of the opposite sex and the subsequent objectification of the gazed-upon. Boy bands develop because there is a vociferous demand for satisfying the sexual appetite of teenage girls—an appetite that is only allowed expression in safe, "harmless" ways. The idea that "One Direction exists to teach girls to look to men for validation" is too simple a reading of the complex and complicated relationship the teen girl gaze has with celebrity. Being a fan of a boy band is, for teen girls, a safe way to explore sexual desires and to develop a confident method of understanding oneself and one's own body.

To say boy bands are a method of teaching women to cater to the male gaze, as critics of One Direction have argued, is to simplify the larger cultural exchange happening between the band and their thousands of screaming fans—it is to remove agency from the spectator and place it solely in the hands of the artist. The truth is somewhere in between, where desire, experience, affection, and gaze all interact on a microlevel. Each Directioner harbors the hope of having their gaze returned by the band member of their affection—they want to see themselves as the object of that singer's affection. But the singers themselves aren't solely gazing at their fans—they are also engaged in a return and an encouragement of that gaze. The video for "Night Changes" demonstrates this on a metacritical level. In a kind of choose-your-own-adventure montage, each of the five members of the band takes the viewer on a date, from being served wine in a fancy restaurant to having a stroll along the river in a park; there is no "hot model" or "video babe" to be seen—it's just you, the viewer, out with the man of your dreams. The men look directly into the camera, returning the gaze of affection that their fans are placing on them, catering to the fantasies they've been living out for ages.

Both the band and their fan base exist in a mutually sustained relationship: the men cannot have their career without the massive base of teen girls, who return the objectifying gaze as they swoon over the men and explore their own burgeoning sexuality. Thus, boy bands play a significant and fundamental role in the development of how we understand both our own gaze and the gaze of others and what selfhood looks like in the midst of that exchange. One only has to look to the Backstreet Boys' immensely popular *Millennium* album to see how this exchange takes place—the album was dedicated to fans and the first single from it, "Larger than Life," was all about how their massive cadre of female fans made their lives the way they are. The loving gaze of the fans changes the reality of the gazed-upon star.

We cannot engage accurately with all the diversity of representations within popular culture if our methods of interpretation are dependent upon an antiquated idea of entertainment as a one-way street, with an active gazer and a passive receiver. The advent of the internet, of YouTube, of Netflix, of Twitter has changed how we gaze and at what. The "gaze" is still useful in particular instances as shorthand for understanding the overarching culture of male dominance and feminine subservience, but the ongoing conversation between gazes nullifies the age-old thesis that women are merely passive receivers of the male gaze. To say the male gaze is simply objectifying women dehumanizes both artist and fan, leaving neither with proper agency for understanding the particular and peculiar market of objectification and subjectivity that develops in a fan base of mostly teenage girls.

Teen girls are standing up and screaming not just because these men are finally gazing at them, but because they finally have the opportunity to gaze back. It's a chance to explore those fantasies the initial male gaze evokes—and thus it's hard to argue that there isn't something empowering about boy-band fandom and the subsequent ownership of sexuality that accompanies such fanaticism. Nothing demonstrated this better than Harry Styles's eponymous album release as a solo artist. Styles's album—a critical masterpiece that crosses genre boundaries and is an immense debut—launched him into a tour that sold out almost immediately. But the tour was very different from the usual multimillion-selling album promotional tour. Instead of big stadiums with thousands in the audience, Styles elected to play smaller clubs that could hold only a few hundred people. Each show, Styles determined, would be a small, intimate group so that his fans could have a more genuine experience with the music and the work. This decision to deliberately eschew the millions in profit he could have made on a stadium tour is yet more evidence that the space between the fan and the artist is an intimate, closely held exchange that is not merely about the male artist imposing his gaze upon female fans.

Perhaps one of the best ways to explicate this gazer–gazed-upon paradox in popular music is to look not to a male artist, but to a female one. In 2012 singer Carly Rae Jepsen showed up with a ridiculously catchy and sugary sweet pop anthem, "Call Me Maybe." In the video (and as the singer of the song), Jepsen takes on the traditionally male role of gazing upon and objectifying her crush. She attempts to catch his gaze, washing her car in a manner perhaps perceived as "sexy" in some alternate universe. She is craving that objectifying gaze she has pushed upon him throughout the video—but it's not working out that way. The disappointment when the object of her affection turns out to have an interest in the same sex is comical because it's a refutation of both forms of the gaze—her desire to be the object of his consumptive gaze, and her consumptive gaze toward him. It's a rebuke of the idea that we exist for the gaze of others—because they have lives of their own. It's complex gaze theory in a catchy pop song!

Popular music itself is the dark horse of political, feminist criticism—there's an entire underground discourse happening throughout the Top Forty that many critics dismiss outright, simply because it is popular. It is the kind of thing my baby niece will nod her head to, which, for some reason, undermines its weightiness in a critical world. But even in its sugary sweetness, the exchange between popular music and teenage fandom is continually adjusting and challenging our vision of ourselves and how and who we gaze upon. We are living and existing within a multifaceted, paradoxical world that can no longer be explained by a simple psychoanalytic theory of an active viewer and a passive object. We are more than what makes us beautiful and we are actually encouraged to own our sexuality through fandom of various boy bands and artists. One Direction is not a plague upon the music world, but rather a natural outgrowth of the meeting of young male and female sexuality, developing alongside each other, gazing back and forth and developing their own understandings of themselves.

3

On My Money and
Bitches Who Better Have It

How Modern Anticapitalists Fail to Account
for Racial Politics of Black Artists

Following the outcome of the 2016 presidential election, red roses began popping up in usernames all over Twitter. The symbolism was at once an "I told you so" from people who supported the self-identified socialist Bernie Sanders in the Democrat primaries and a way of signaling to other socialists on the platform that you "got it," you're "in the know." The word "neoliberal" entered the layperson's lexicon and suddenly everyone I knew was an expert on Marxist and Leninist theory. Unfortunately, proponents of socialism and those frustrated with it seemed to run along a harsh divide: many of the socialists were white, cisgender men and women. Those targeted and aggravated by the massive "I told you so" campaign were mostly women of color. This ongoing divide has brought to light the remarkable failings of a Marxist socialist lens on societal structure.

Marxism is a scary word for a lot of people—they associate Marxism with communism and communism with dictatorial regimes in which freedoms are restricted and people are thrown in jail for speaking out against their government. In the 1950s and '60s, at the height of the Cold War, discussing Marxism or Marxist critique was a frightening prospect, even for academics who used the theories in literary criticism. McCarthyism cracked down on strains of communist and Marxist thought by blacklisting and engaging in a witch hunt that targeted many famous people as having communist sympathies. The Cold War taught us, over and over again, that socialism, communism, and Marxism were essentially the same thing and that all were anti-American ideologies. It's very hard to discuss the important critique Marxism brings to the table without the argument devolving into the fear that gripped America during the Cold War. The very word scares off a lot of otherwise engaged people. And the hostile nature that many Marxists and socialists bring to their critiques adds to the stigma and consternation surrounding the philosophy.

So we need to get a couple of things straight: when I say Marxist, I'm referring to the historical method of criticism and critique of capitalist structure, not making a political statement that capitalism should be replaced by a totalitarian regime (which is not what Marxism is anyway). Marxism is actually a lens of critique, not a system in and of itself. *Marxist* as a word is a descriptor, not a prescriptive action. It comes from the critiques of capitalism put forward by Karl Marx and his friend and benefactor Friedrich Engels, and it argues that inequality of class within the capitalist system is explained by looking at who controls the means of production and the money that is garnered through that production. Marxism argues that an examination of how the means of production are controlled and who possesses what property is an important indicator of oppression and of what direction that oppression flows. In other words, Marxism tells us to follow the money to find where the oppressor lies. There are a lot of ideological, feminist points in Marxism that many people would probably support if they weren't labeled as Marxism. Perhaps it all comes down to a branding issue.

Marxist feminism, as an activist view, criticizes the system of capitalism itself as oppressive to marginalized bodies. In capitalism, those who labor, those who run the means of production, have no share in the profits of that production. Think, for example, of the searing report in *Mother Jones* on Amazon.com's warehouse labor, where people work in sweltering, almost inhumane conditions, for very little pay. Meanwhile, CEO Jeff Bezos makes millions, if not billions, for running the business. Capitalism dictates that profit motive is necessarily a moral good and that a free market for goods means a free citizenry. This removes human compassion from the reigning economic system—money is the only measure of good.

Marxism argues that those who create the goods should have shares in their profit. Under capitalism, however, those who own the means of production own all. Marxism rejects that idea of ownership and of private property altogether, arguing that a world in which money is the determining factor of the good is a world corrupted. Marx himself was poor most of his life, borrowing money frequently from his friend Engels and dependent upon the emotional and domestic labor of his wife and daughters in order to survive. In other words, a pure Marxism might not be a great way to function, as Marx's own life shows us. But the Marxist critique of the capitalist system still holds a lot of weight, particularly its criticism of money being the sole factor in determining moral good. It's a critique that surfaces again and again in the engagement with the commercialized nature of popular culture.

One of the most salient examples of this critique appears in a discussion of the musical goddess Beyoncé. In 2016 pop artist Beyoncé released *Lemonade*, an album about, by, and for black women. The accompanying visual album aired on a Saturday night on the premium cable channel HBO. For the first twenty-four hours, the album was available only on an exclusive streaming service that required credit card information in order to listen. It was exclusively available to people who had the funds to watch, a masterful marketing strategy but one that may not be so feminist. Feminist theorist and author bell hooks criticized Beyoncé for this move, arguing, essentially, that women participating in a capitalist system in the way that Beyoncé does are actively harming the women they are supposedly aiming to help. She wrote on her website:

Viewers who like to suggest *Lemonade* was created solely or primarily for black female audiences are missing the point. Commodities, irrespective of their subject matter, are made, produced, and marketed to entice any and all consumers. Beyoncé's audience is the world and that world of business and money-making has no color.[1]

She goes on to argue that *Lemonade* exploits black female pain for profit, offering not a solution or empowerment for black women but a "positive exploit[action]" of the black female body for capitalist gain. This capitalism, this method of commercializing art, is what hooks objects to.

Of course, hooks is right in a lot of ways. Capitalism is very bad for women. Women are more likely to live in poverty in the United States. We're more likely to stay in terrible, hostile work environments because we're more often single mothers. We're more likely to be employed in low-wage retail and fast-food jobs where the fight rages for a livable minimum wage. We're also more likely to be paid less than our male counterparts—a statistical gap that increases once you add race, ability, and body size into the equation. A fat Latina makes far less on average than a skinny white woman for the same job.

We're also more often expected to pick up domestic labor once we get home from our low-paying jobs. While the number of (white) women working outside the home has drastically increased since the mid-twentieth century, the division of domestic labor between men and women has remained approximately the same. Many women are still expected to cook dinner for their families and clean the house after returning home from their low-wage jobs. Capitalism, as a system that builds up the wealth of white men, does so to the detriment of women.

Popular music is one of the places where female artists are able to shine. Unfortunately, they do so by participating in that same capitalist structure that holds a lot of women down. Beyoncé's team has made a conscious effort to combat that: she hires women of color and centers the work of women of color both in front of and behind the camera. In the *Lemonade* visual album, white people are few and far between—women of color, specifically black women, fill each and every scene, dancing in clothing of traditional African designs, invoking Cajun and Southern imagery throughout the short film. The mothers of black men killed at the hands of police appear in a moving tribute; black women are front and center, and their work is highlighted by Beyoncé's work in raising the profile of black women. She might be called, in Republican parlance, a job creator. But there's an ideological debate as to whether this participation in capitalism makes her a problematic feminist.

Hooks contends that such participation absolutely makes her problematic. Hooks writes that Beyoncé's feminism is shallow, predicated on violence and a weak understanding of equality between men and women. It is violent because she participates in capitalism. It is shallow because she uses Chimamanda Ngozi Adichie's understanding of a feminist as a person who believes in the "social, political and economic equality of the sexes," which some criticize as being far too simple an aphorism for explaining the entirety of the lens of feminism. She laments that Beyoncé lacks an intersectional lens in her feminist discussion, even as Beyoncé emphasizes her identity as a black woman oppressed by patriarchal and white supremacist ideas of who she is supposed to be. In other words, hooks here is providing us with a perfect example of how a critique of art can go awry—there's nothing Beyoncé can do that would be good enough for hooks's extremely high standard, which rejects any capitalist structure involving the black female body. Hooks wants perfection, and Beyoncé cannot give it.

The irony here, of course, is that hooks offers her critique from the position of an academic, which brings forward its own issues of accessibility and participation in a system of oppression. Academics have the tendency to imagine themselves as above or beyond the normal fray of systems, able to critique others from their ivory tower without ever entering into it with the riffraff. When I began my Women's Studies degree, this question was at the forefront—we were, after all, sitting in a lecture room in one of the oldest and most expensive (and expansive) libraries in the United Kingdom, having access to that which very few people are able to reach. The exclusivity of such access does give academics a kind of artificial high—there's nothing quite like being able to swipe a card and enter an exclusive club that most people will never get to see. And hooks, while cognizant of her own position, seems willing to give herself grace for participating in the capitalist system while refusing to extend Beyoncé that same leeway.

Hooks's critique comes from an important theory-centered place, however. It is important to question the role money plays in guiding what we see as art and what gets preserved as canon. The fact that women could not own property and could not sell the rights to their work for many years has led to the erasure of women's artistry from history. Art has long been guided by money, with wealthy patrons commissioning artists. Much of the art we have in museums exists because someone paid for it. This relationship of capitalism to art brings contradiction to the role of art within society—art can be used to push, to radicalize, to rebel. But when it must be tied to a patron, to a money-making scheme, the presence of money naturally tempers some art, as the artist may need to continue to be paid and therefore to continue to eat.

When rubber meets road, there's an important decision to be made about feminist activism. I've had these conversations myself, where I have to decide if I am an activist or an author and if there's any way these two facts about my life can align. Every single woman who wants to be active in the liberation of women has to ask this question, and it's no different for women participating in popular culture. Indeed, those women with platforms that speak to millions may be under a greater obligation to take this decision seriously, asking themselves what they can do for feminism as a celebrity. And celebrities, by their nature, are constructs necessary to capitalism.

Beyoncé clearly takes this decision under consideration, as she attempts to do multiple things at once in engaging her black identity, her womanhood, and her status as a pop icon. She is famously a micromanager of her image, keeping a vault of every appearance, every performance, every magazine cover. She uses her position as a famous singer to encourage black women to take control of their lives, to own who they are, to feel their anger, their sadness, their experiences with realism, not shoving them away and pretending to be perfect. And, no question, she focuses at least part of her work on her money.

Beyoncé focuses on capitalistic gain as a form of revenge against a system that calls her worthless solely on the basis of her being a black woman. Throughout her career, she talks about how black women making money and earning their own way through life is a form of subversive action. In "Run the World (Girls)" and "Formation," Beyoncé instructs her legions of black female fans to use their capitalist gains, their ability to pay their own way, as revenge against a system that wants them dependent on others.

In Beyoncé's world, the use of capitalism as a response to marginalization is a sensible one. It says to people who think worth is measured by dollars and by how well a person can play the capitalist game, "I'm better than you at this. Don't even try." For a black woman from a traditionally marginalized and impoverished culture, the ability to be at once at the same level as rich, oppressive white people and yet still be on the outside is a great benefit and a great pain. By taking a typically white supremacist culture of pop music and being unapologetically black, Beyoncé makes a huge statement.

But the question does remain about whether or not this is a moral good—is participating in the commercial system, even if you're better at it, even if you're using it *for good* and to be a model of empowerment for women, a good thing?

The behavior of teenage girls in response to capitalist structures is a significant marker of how we can measure and complicate the morality of money and commercial goods in a world full of oppressive structures. In a remarkable 2016 feature for *Good* magazine, writer Tasbeeh Herwees investigates the world of teenage girls who "lift." Not weightlifting, but shoplifting. Many of the girls—the majority of whom are white, middle-class girls in their midteen years—identify a fight back against capitalism as a motivation and justification for why they steal. One lifter articulates her stealing habit as a method of feminist resistance: "Being a teen girl is hard—you have to be skinny, attractive, put together, well dressed, etc. Society teaches girls through media and the beauty industry that they need to be perfect. . . . I'm sick of handing my money over to corporations that profit on this bullshit . . . so if I have to put up with this kind of stuff, I'm certainly not going to pay for it."[2] Capitalism is often seen by feminists as a system in which we are trapped, from which there is no escape. So these teenagers moralize that they are doing an ultimate good by stealing from stores that act in oppressive ways. This simplistic view of corporate evil allows the teens to brush aside the real-life consequences of their crimes—which is that some poor retail worker is probably going to get fired over missing inventory from their store. Writer Paul Baker argues that this narrow view of capitalism as an ultimate evil is lacking nuance:

> There is no reason why capitalist structures always have to rely on strictly hegemonic discourses. Within post-modern thinking, there is recognition that a range of possible identities and discourses exist, and while it is still the case that other identities are subordinated or marginalized to hegemonic masculinity, at the same time, advertisers are aware that people possessing these "bothered" identities still have money to spend and choices to make about where to spend it. The relationship between commodification and non-hegemonic identities or discourses is a complex one.[3]

Because men are not the only ones participating in the capitalist system, being able to monetize differing identities is an important move for corporations and capitalist enterprise. It isn't just a one-way street of oppressive hegemony anymore. It's a complex relationship. Can we say, then, that our relationship to capitalism can be one of good, of benefit, in some ways? Can we disrupt the system through the assertion of our marginalized identities within a commercial space?

Many progressives say no, exhibiting a form of ideological purity that argues that money is a corrupting influence and forces many to do immoral things in order to survive. But this kind of ideological purity ends up being a critique based in good old-fashioned misogyny. Making money at something you're good at, in this anticapitalist ideology, means that you've sold out, that you've gone capitalist and are therefore participating in a bad system—especially if you're a woman and already under increased scrutiny. This leads to the false idea that the only real activists are the poor ones, the ones struggling to survive. The only good artist is a starving one. This argument takes critical aim at the wrong subjects, blaming the individual activist for the faults of the system.

This view of valorizing non-money-making actions devalues the labor of women. Many of the feminists working themselves to the bone for the feminist cause are women, and by arguing that we should not make more money or participate in commercialized systems as a method of survival, we devalue female labor—labor that is already devalued in our culture. We may be trying to say that our labor is *too* valuable to participate in a corporatist marketplace, but the end result is that the labor of women is valued only insofar as it doesn't make money—which results in a net gain of exactly nothing. In our efforts to exact revenge on a capitalist structure, we harm the very people we're trying to save from capitalism. Bell hooks, in her desire to hold Beyoncé to a higher standard in which the commodification of black female bodies is stopped, ends up missing the forest for the trees: she dismisses Beyoncé's hard work and the labor that goes into the consciousness raising that she does, all because she does so in the form of a commercial album and video that sells copies. This critique is all too familiar for famous women deemed problematic.

In 2015 R&B artist Rihanna released a long-form video for her then single "Bitch Better Have My Money." In the video, she takes the wife of her accountant hostage in order to exact revenge upon him for stealing money from her over the course of years. The entire story is based on a real-life battle with Rihanna's own accountant, who stole millions of dollars from her after being entrusted with her accounts when she was a young pop star. Rihanna was seventeen when her first big album came out. In the video, nearly a decade later, she is able to exact the revenge denied her in real life, creating a literal bloodbath as she tortures and kills her "accountant," played by actor Mads Mikkelsen. In the closing scenes of the video, she is literally covered in blood, lounging in a trunk full of money. The gauntlet has been thrown: she will not be devalued or taken advantage of again.

Many criticized the video as problematic—she attacks a white woman as part of her effort for revenge, which many saw not as a revenge fantasy but as a misogynistic treatment of women's bodies. In making that critique, many—like bell hooks with Beyoncé's *Lemonade*—missed the forest for the trees. Rihanna asserts that greed and sexism and racism seem to go hand in hand—and the manifestation of that intersecting oppression is in the fact that she, as a black woman, is not seeing the dues she deserves for the work she does as an artist. Rihanna asserts her right to the valuation of her labor in a visually shocking manner, but her point cannot be missed: her labor is worthwhile and she deserves accurate compensation for such work. Bitch, she's getting her money.

As much as we want to critique the capitalist system as oppressive and misogynistic, we also still must work under it, because it is the system as it stands. We're not going to have a Marxist revolt of the proletariat any time soon, which is why pushing for progressive purity in action and ideology among individual artists, as though they were responsible for reforming entire systems, is foolish at best and dangerously misplaced at worst. Reforming systems cannot fall to Beyoncé any more than you or I can move a mountain.

It's important, too, to recognize that the bulk of these critiques about feminist purity fall upon women. No one is calling for Rage Against the Machine to give up their money in order to fall in line with progressive politics, despite their politically charged work. Female artists, particularly female artists of color, are the ones who are told they must not receive adequate compensation for their labor. In order to be a true feminist, you cannot make money off the work you perform and put your life into. Rather than supporting adequate compensation for labor, current Marxist critique toward women of color devalues their labor and their work, demanding that they fall in line with rejecting capitalist systems.

So Beyoncé uses her feminism to sell albums. She shouldn't do this, as a feminist, however, because of some vague idea about how feminists—mostly women—should not take part in a capitalist system that puts so many women in poverty.

But if we stand by that ideological purity, we cannot participate in feminist discourse altogether. Everything is touched by capitalist hands. The tweets we send are the product of a publicly traded company. That email service you use to organize your life and work is likewise from a billion-dollar industry. *There is no way to participate in an activist feminism without also engaging in a capitalist structure, because capitalism is part and parcel of our daily lives.* What this ideological, Marxist purity demands is that we must live off grid entirely in order to engage in activism properly. But even then, if we're white American feminists, we're living on land stolen in the name of capitalist manifest destiny, which means even our off-grid, non-commercialized culture is still part of a capitalist, colonialist enterprise.

There is no escape.

So what, then, are we to do? We live within a system in which moral quality is determined by monetary gain, and we engage in an idealism that places progressive values at the forefront of a moral good. How do we reconcile the two in a manner that does not devalue the labor of the marginalized?

We stop pushing for ideological purity on the part of people who share our values. One of the values of progressivism actually contradicts the desire for such ideological purity—the prizing of diverse voices, and the centering of the marginalized, demands that we don't hold our fellow progressives to untenable standards of ideological purity. We have to step back and realize that sometimes the message is more important than the means, though the means is not insignificant. We can either have a Beyoncé who proclaims feminism and the power of women at every turn and makes money doing so, or we can have artists who buy into the starving artist ideal and are only heard from by a few. Efforts to avoid the problematic are in themselves problematic.

However, this doesn't necessarily mean giving up the fight. There's a delicate balance that has to be made: we cannot begrudge artists for creating work within the system of capitalism and making money to feed their family while doing it. Perhaps Beyoncé's method of approaching the issue is a good example: while she makes money doing commercialized work, she creates art that has great value for her listeners and encourages an understanding of their role within an oppressive system, speaking up for and empowering them. With the money that she makes from these endeavors, she donates to and supports progressive causes. During the Black Lives Matter protests in Ferguson, Missouri, following the death of Michael Brown at the hands of police, Beyoncé and her husband, rapper Jay-Z, used their substantial wealth to bail protestors out of prison. They recognized that their significant wealth put them in a position to help others, and they gave generously, not for publicity, but to genuinely support causes they believe in.

The symbols themselves are meaningful. To complain about the money artists make is to devalue the symbolic importance of that art. When Beyoncé marched into the Super Bowl in 2016 with a veritable army of women dressed in Black Panther gear, the symbolism of that moment was unmistakable and moving—even if it happened in the middle of the giant capitalist circle jerk that is the Super Bowl.

They helped where they could while recognizing that the system itself still needed to change—which is what led to the New Orleans-centered music video for "Formation," with Beyoncé dancing on top of a police car and featuring a small child dancing in front of riot police in a hoodie. Despite engaging with a capitalist system, much of the work Beyoncé does with her music and her advocacy challenges that system. She is creating art that rebels, that inspires, that revolutionizes.

We live in a capitalist system, which carries with it a number of attendant problems. But that doesn't mean we give up and live off the grid, nor does it mean we uncritically embrace the system. We must continue to work to change the system in which we are living, while recognizing that we do live here. We may not overturn an entire system within our lifetime, but we can use our critical faculties to make good decisions about which artists and which cultures we choose to support, even if it means engaging with a system that is, at its roots, problematic.

4

Why Does This White Australian Sound like She's from Atlanta?

On Cultural Appropriation, White Supremacy, and Black Sexuality

In a strange departure from my typical no-kids, no-marriage approach to life, I worked at a daycare center for a brief time in my late twenties. Like any job, I got along with some coworkers and not with others. Unfortunately, the one I didn't get along with was my pseudo "dotted line" boss. She didn't trust my ability to do basic math in counting the children left on the playground, even though the owner of the daycare had assigned that task to me. She consistently undermined my authority with the kids, calling my orders into question only to turn around and give the exact same command. She was fond of calling the little boys her "boyfriends" and signified which kid was her favorite by announcing who her boyfriend was that week. As a feminist, I had a lot of trouble with placing such signifiers of relationships on children so tiny—it has the accidental effect of teaching children that grooming behaviors like having secrets and "adult girlfriends" are totally okay.

But perhaps most needling was a personality quirk that just irked me to no end. She was super fond of the rapper Iggy Azalea, so every time we were out on the playground, she'd inevitably burst into "I'M SO FAN-CEEE" and the song would be stuck in my head for the rest of the day. For me, in those moments, her shout-singing on the playground was a microcosm of everything I felt was wrong with her as a fellow white woman. Iggy Azalea is a white Australian from a wealthy background who raps in what many critics have referred to as a "blaccent" or "black accent." Particularly, she adopts a tone and method of rapping that reflects African American Vernacular English. In her top hit "Fancy," her blaccent is obvious from the first lines. The *Washington Post* said of Azalea's fame: "For a spell, Iggy Azalea was the Donald Trump of the rap game: racially divisive, prone to ugly rants—and confoundingly popular."[1]

The increasingly visible appropriation of African American vernacular and cultural cues and signifiers by white artists has also made the discussion about representation come to the forefront. Scholars such as Tressie McMillan Cottom and Flavia Dzodan have written extensively about the problems of white culture consuming black culture—whiteness turns blackness into a game, something palatable and fun to play with and try on while simultaneously denying the ongoing systemic racism and oppression black people face. Cultural appropriation is a method of taking the "fun" of a culture without any of the history or weight of that same culture.

One of the ways in which this cultural appropriation—and acceptance thereof—acts itself out in the popular culture scene is the response to presentations of sexuality and sexualized bodies. A white woman who takes on blackness for fun, who appropriates dance forms, styles, and ideas from black culture plays with her sexuality in ways inaccessible to the black women who invented these signifiers in the first place. From Iggy Azalea to Miley Cyrus, from Nicki Minaj to Angel Haze, female sexuality plays out in significantly different ways, leading a white feminist standard of "sexual liberation" to become incoherent in the face of our actual historical context.

One of the most viewed music videos of 2013 was a release from former Disney Channel star Miley Cyrus. In a strikingly beautiful sequence, shot by Terry Richardson (a man frequently accused of sexual misconduct on his photography sets) Cyrus appears fully nude except for some Doc Marten boots. Her new short hair with a buzzed undercut and her striking red lips covering brilliantly white teeth make for a particularly compelling aesthetic. She swings back and forth on a large wrecking ball that's a bit on the nose, considering the song is literally titled "Wrecking Ball."

Her 2013 album *Bangerz* was a major departure from her Disneyfied, family-friendly image. By pairing up with a photographer who is noted for his particularly lascivious behavior, she took a leap with presenting her sexuality to the world as a *woman*, no longer a girl under the thumb of the rules of a sexual culture demanding purity and modesty. She has since commented that she regrets her behavior, returning once again to the clean, white-washed, if not prim, vision of white femininity.[2]

Or, at least, if you listened to white feminist media in those days, that's what you heard. Cyrus's sudden turnaround and debut of her new selfhood were remarkable, and the talk of the web for months. Miley Cyrus's tongue was the cultural icon of 2013: the symbol of sexual liberation. And toward the end of 2015, the UK website The Tab declared that Miley Cyrus was "the only feminist icon we need in 2016." The site offered this as justification: "She does what she wants when she wants and she wears whatever the fuck she wants whilst doing it," concluding that "when people write about 21st-century feminism, they're writing about Miley."[3]

But at the same time, when Nicki Minaj's derriere became the topic of discussion with the release of her video for "Anaconda," the wider cultural discussion was far less about sexual liberation and much more about being an overtly sexualized woman who is a "bad role model" for women. The stark popular response is symbolic of this divide between cultural appropriative white feminists and the actual feminist work done by black women artists.

Minaj's work is not significantly different from Cyrus's in terms of how it expresses sexuality. Indeed, Minaj's video in many ways is more feminist and engaged in sexual liberation than Cyrus's naked swinging on a wrecking ball. Minaj uses her position in popular culture to engage with and denounce a white culture that regards black female bodies with fear and disgust; Cyrus uses sexual tropes about the pure white woman to shock people. Where Cyrus's work caters to a culture that rewards objectified sexuality, Minaj claps back at a racist, sexist culture that says her body only exists for their consumption.

White women in popular culture are often seen as "in control" of their sexuality, even as they perform it obviously for shock value. Miley Cyrus grinding against Robin Thicke, the singer of the rape-y anthem "Blurred Lines," is sexually liberated. But Nicki Minaj, performing a lap dance for Drake and singing about having sex with men in their cars, is somehow engaging in objectification and oppression of women. Minaj is a victim of sexualization, while Cyrus is "in charge."

All of this discussion that has been bubbling under the surface of music criticism for the past few years has long historical precedent built out of white supremacist myths about female sexuality, both white and black. Patricia Hill Collins, a womanist writer and theorist, writes of the "controlling images" that are used to control and demean black women. These images developed in the Jim Crow–era South when literal ownership and control over the lives of black people was no longer legal. White supremacist culture created methods to defend racist actions against black people by proclaiming that black people had specific problems or sins that put them at fault if they were lynched or attacked. Black women are subject to very specific and contradictory images of who they are: they are the sexless mammy, built to take care of white children and nothing else. They are the tempting Jezebel, built to draw white men away from fidelity to their marriages to pure white women. They are the welfare queen, taking hard-earned white money from the taxpayer to subsidize their lazy lifestyle. Or they are the super-strong black mother, the matriarch of the family, built to undergo any and all forms of suffering, to forgive their child's killers on the national stage within hours of their deaths.

White women, in that same Jim Crow era, were also subject to patriarchal ideas, but these moved in the opposite direction: white women were innocent and pure, lacking any and all sexuality, victims of male predation. They were the foil to the alleged black female promiscuity—pure and precious and holy and inviolable. Their word against the black man was taken as gospel, and many black men were lynched and destroyed by the husbands of white women proclaiming to have been violated. Even the appearance of impropriety toward white women was a death sentence for black men in the lynching era. Emmett Till allegedly whistled at a white woman while at a corner store. He was found days later, floating in a river, tied to a seventy-pound fan stolen from a cotton gin.

All of this forms the background of how we approach and monetize female sexuality in contemporary popular culture. The conflict between Nicki Minaj and Miley Cyrus is just one further example of these controlling images exerting power over our national discourse. Making a decision to praise Miley Cyrus's sexuality and to condemn Nicki Minaj's is not a neutral position based on artistic merit, but one that has deep roots in racist misogyny.

Minaj's body of work clearly positions women as people in control of their sexuality and their bodies—and that, ultimately, is what scares people. She and her entourage assert themselves as strong, powerful women, challenging the audience to see them differently, to see them as whole unique beings, rather than consuming them with sexual lust. Her entire work is essentially a wink at the viewer, a mockery of the stereotypes and images placed upon her shoulders as a woman of color in hip-hop. And the "Anaconda" video is a response to all those ideas about who can and cannot be sexually liberated on the popular culture stage. Taking the hook from rapper Sir Mix-A-Lot's ode to the black female booty—"Baby Got Back"—Minaj sang about her own substantial rear, declaring her own sexual prowess and sexiness. The video is set in an obviously fake jungle, playing on the "Anaconda" reference, and features only Nicki and her crew of women in increasingly hilarious scenarios that emphasize their behinds.

Henry Louis Gates Jr., in a 1990s op-ed about 2 Live Crew, coined the term "sexual carnivalesque." This phrase perfectly encapsulates Minaj's winking attitude toward the commercial reception of her image and her brand of sexuality. The video itself is a carnival. The exaggerated dancing, the use of slow-motion to catch every bounce, every twerk, the jungle setting, and the barely concealed euphemistic fruit all contribute to a video that is *comedic* rather than sexually objectifying.

Throughout the video, Minaj meets the gaze of the viewer, unblinking, knowingly laughing at the reaction she's sure to get. She at once mocks and embraces the idea that she is present as a sexual commodity, purposefully drawing the viewer in and then cutting them off, asserting her boundaries to her own body. She dares you to objectify her.

It's all a farce, an ongoing mockery of those controlling images that turn Minaj into a sexual object for white male consumption.

In one particularly entrancing scene in the "Anaconda" video, Minaj dances behind a counter in a French maid outfit, spraying whipped cream on her breasts and pretending to cook. At one point, she imitates fellatio on a banana, only to grab a knife in the next second and cut off the tip. The message is clear: her sexual performance is on her terms, and her terms alone.

So in the fall of 2015, when "Anaconda" failed to be nominated for the MTV Video of the Year Award, Minaj was rightfully offended—her work was unique, interesting, and added to the conversation about female sexuality in the mainstream. Not to mention it had millions of views on YouTube and was one of the most popular videos of the year. She tweeted that the category—which only had one black woman, Minaj's friend Beyoncé, in it—seemed to be only available to skinny women. Taylor Swift, a fellow artist who was nominated, took the commentary personally, responding that Minaj was "pitting women against each other."[4] The two managed to talk it over and come to an understanding, but not before other white, female, pop artists formed opinions and spouted off in the press. Cyrus, who was hosting the MTV Video Music Awards that year, commented days before the ceremony that Minaj was not being polite and was just thinking about herself.

Cyrus's comments invoked the respectability politics that have governed the relationship between activist black people and the oppressive white ruling class for generations. If a black person doesn't speak up in "appropriate" or "respectable" ways, then they can be dismissed because they did not fit into a narrowly acceptable tone. The only good black person in respectability politics is the one who takes on whiteness—they are subservient, determined to be perceived as "respectable." It's highly likely that Cyrus was unaware of what historical precedents she was invoking when she said those things about Minaj in the New York Times. But she stepped into it anyway.

Minaj didn't miss a beat, and in the comment heard round the world, she called Cyrus out directly from the stage at the VMAs after accepting a different award: "And now back to this bitch who had a lot to say about me the other day in the press. Miley, what's good?"

On the surface and in plain text, her comment doesn't read as much of a zinger. But in the context of the moment, she was challenging both the commentary that Cyrus had made about her "politeness" and asking her to step up to the plate if this was a discussion she was going to engage in. It was an open, public clapback, definitively closing the book on the matter. She later explained that she was tired of Cyrus using black culture and black language to promote her white agenda and to explore her sexuality.

This, exactly, is the rub.

The plain fact of the matter is that white feminist criticism sets a much higher bar for acceptance of black artists, particularly if their work trades in evoking a sexual response. Miley Cyrus gets multiple chances to fuck up, but Beyoncé has to be perfect in everything. Taylor Swift is forgiven for everything, but Nicki Minaj can never get angry or upset. What's more is that white pop artists frequently base their careers on the appropriation and stealing of cultural ideas and musical tropes invented within black culture.

This is most obvious in Miley Cyrus's video for "We Can't Stop," the first single from *Bangerz*. In the video, a thin, luminescently pale Cyrus dances around with large black women, twerking against their butts, slapping them and essentially using them as objects for her enjoyment. We don't see their faces—they're just asses, shaking at the camera. Black cultural cues are everywhere. Cyrus puts a grill on her teeth, wears a shirt that reads "DOPE" (which is African American Vernacular English slang), wears a slouchy hat and makes hand gestures at the camera that originated within hip-hop. The appropriation of black symbols without attribution or the autonomous, active presence of black bodies removes these symbols from their context and turns them into playthings for Miley's amusement.

This kind of cultural appropriation is common within white American culture—black musical culture is a playground for white artists, where artists show up and take what they want, regardless of where or how it originated, taking it for their own. In contrast to Minaj, whose cultural cues in her videos pay tribute both to American black and her native Trinidadian cultures, Cyrus's contextless playing around with language and cultural symbols dishonors their original meanings and dishonors the culture they came from. It is another form of asserting supremacy over black people—even their culture does not and cannot exist without people stealing from them.

The deliberate dismissal of cultural appropriation among white artists by critics contributes to the ongoing oppression and lack of acceptance of black women in the entertainment industry. When Miley Cyrus performed at the Video Music Awards in 2013 and brought fat black women out onto the stage to be her backup dancers, it took black sociological critic Tressie McMillan Cottom to explain that this *wasn't* a body-positive feminist move:

Fat non-normative black female bodies are kith and kin with historical caricatures of black women as work sites, production units, subjects of victimless sexual crimes and embodied deviance. . . . Playing the desirability of black female bodies as a "wink-wink" joke is a way of lifting up our deviant sexuality without lifting up black women as equally desirable to white women. Cyrus did not just have black women gyrating behind her. She had particularly rotund black women. She gleefully slaps the ass of one dancer like she intends to eat it on a cracker. She is playing a type of black female body as a joke to challenge her audience's perceptions of herself while leaving their perceptions of black women's bodies firmly intact. It's a dance between performing sexual freedom and maintaining a hierarchy of female bodies from which white women benefit materially.[5]

It was only after black women's voices were taken seriously by white critics that a racial lens even came into play in discussion of white female sexual liberation. For white women, sexual liberation was the core and center of a feminist liberative movement, which, as discussed in chapter 1, is part of what divides feminism and womanism as movements and theories. This divide continues to act itself out in the ways in which we embrace or critique female sexuality.

The fact of the matter is that black female bodies, when placed in sexual situations in popular culture, are more likely to be criticized as overtly sexual or even pornographic. White female artists "explore" sexuality while black female artists "objectify themselves." Pink can dance around in nothing but a bralette and underwear, but God forbid Beyoncé dance around in a leotard.

By the same token, white artists can play with queerness in ways inaccessible to black women. Toying with queerness is a common trope in popular culture, starting in the millennial generation when the Russian pop group t.A.T.u.'s two female singers made out with each other in their music video, and then denied any claim to queer identity. The performance of lesbianism is common throughout all elements of popular culture—from Katy Perry singing about kissing a girl to Madonna and Britney Spears kissing at the MTV Video Music Awards. But the majority of the jokes about this trope are confined to white artists who have the veneer of being "appropriately" sexual to back them up, should anyone actually suspect that they may be queer. They're just playing, and this playfulness is open to them because they are white.

Black women, already tarred with a brush proclaiming them deviant jezebels, don't get to engage in the performative lesbianism that white women have access to—at least not in popular culture. The amount of criticism levied at black women for their "natural" sexuality prevents identification of their intersectional identities if they are actually queer. White women, with a blank slate of sexuality, can play with the performance of queerness readily and easily.

All of this comes to bear on how sexuality acts out between famous people of different races. One of the most famous examples of how white women are able to play on both innocence and sexuality at the same moment is within the person of Taylor Swift. Bursting onto the country music scene at seventeen with songs that bashed other women and were built on pseudo-conservative morality, she was at once a darling of the pop world and a target of feminist ire. Over the years, she's developed an image that captures some feminist credentials and gives her an image as a more nuanced thinker and contributor to the conversations about women in popular culture. In her 2015 album, titled *1989*, after her birth year, she sends up popular narratives about her dating life in a song called "Blank Space." The title is a sly reference to how the media treats her like she has a "blank space" behind her name: "Taylor Swift and [fill in the name here]."

But in the same moment, she's used her white femaleness as a shield against numerous criticisms. She's never really grasped the ability to check her own privilege as a white person—as a woman, she gets and understands this particular vector of oppression. But her own analysis never quite extends beyond that, which allows her to continue playing the dual role of "feminist" darling while stepping over black people to get there.

Her long and extended beef with Kanye West and now West's wife, Kim Kardashian-West, explicates this tendency to favor white women's feelings over the oppression they perpetuate. Way back in 2009, rapper Kanye West hopped up on stage to interrupt Swift as she was receiving the award for video of the year at the MTV Video Music Awards over the head of Beyoncé. West's brash and unexpected mic-grab was immediately turned into a meme for the world to laugh at: "Imma let you finish, but . . ." But in the midst of that meme was a real struggle of a woman seeking validation in the world of music and having that validation torn from her and turned into a joke. The "beef" between Kanye and Taylor became the stuff of legends, despite numerous proclamations that they had made up.

Until 2015, that is. West released a song called "Famous" in which he referenced his ongoing struggles with Swift. In one line, he used the word "bitch" to describe her. And Swift, with newly minted feminist credentials after her intensely popular 1989 release, called foul, saying she'd not heard the line before and disapproved greatly of West's misogyny. She quickly turned around the situation so that West—already an object of mockery—became the villain persecuting the poor white woman.

This narrative stuck around until it was revealed that Swift's feminist consternation was mostly an act: West had called her up and had her approve the line. She was not—at least not completely—blindsided by the references to her in the song, though she has continued to claim that "bitch" was not in the version West read to her. West's wife, Kim Kardashian, had recorded the original conversation, however, and Swift's performance of feminist consternation and anger was immediately revealed to be a calculated move meant to continue a public feud, rather than genuine feminist criticism. The white woman, leaning into a new feminist media reputation, used her race and her position in a calculated move to bank further on her newfound "feminism." Much like Miley Cyrus attacking Nicki Minaj to make her own name bigger, Swift used cultural sympathy toward white women to get her name back in the news.

The controversy immediately became about something so much bigger than three very rich celebrities. This was a famous black man calling a famous white woman a "bitch" and the famous white woman using tropes about dangerous black men in order to shore up her feminist brand.

This is about as problematic as it gets. And feminist media played right into the story, first by casting Swift as the victim and taking her original criticism of the "bitch" line as an example of feminist thought and outreach.

Then, when it was revealed that Swift had, in fact, approved Kanye's line, media hopped into the fray again, breathlessly revoking her feminist credentials, declaring that she was a racist who wanted to use a black man to get a leg up. She was no longer the feminist darling. The label was as fickle as the Top Forty charts in the middle of summer.

In both cases of media "feuds," whether between Minaj and Cyrus or West and Swift, the media—including feminist media—has played an extremely important role in playing up the controlling images that both parties are responding to and engaging in. Swift and Cyrus both perform the naïve, innocent white woman coming into her own, while West and Minaj are the evil black people who tear away at their innocence and hold them to higher standards.

Media, at large, thrives on this meme of problematization that permeates much of the online feminist discourse. If a person is doing something vaguely feminist, they are suddenly an icon of the new wave of feminist thought. If they fail, they are written off and destroyed in media reputation. All of it is based on consumption and clicks and who can get more people to read and guess at their notorious blind items of gossip about celebrity failures. And this media, including our own self-identified feminist media, uses this swinging metric of public opinion in determining who and what to cover, and what will direct the feminist conversation in the right ways. In playing to the Your Fave Is Problematic cataloguing of sins, our own criticism falls prey to perpetuating decades-old tropes and images of segregation and separation. On all levels, this catalogue of sins and racing after the latest celebrity scandals, these hot takes and think pieces on what it really means that Kanye called Taylor a bitch, contribute to a culture in which one's feminism is ever subject to the wind of public opinion on a particular day. Such problematization and labeling create a world in which serious sins are not taken seriously, because every little thing holds equal weight.

To get ourselves out of this ever critical mindset, we have to remember our subjects. People are human. Celebrities are human. Celebrities are humans surrounded by public relations teams who know how to capitalize on political trends. We have to be smarter in our criticism, learning to differentiate the PR flack from the person themselves, learning to see and understand that one mistake does not a horrible person make. We must refrain from immediate judgment on "problematic" actions and take into account history and ideas and personhood, especially if we are harsher on one person than on another.

We can absolutely have these discussions. We can talk about Iggy Azalea's blaccent. We can talk about Miley Cyrus's tongue. We can defend Nicki Minaj's ass. And we can take pride in Beyoncé's Black Panther–style leotards. But we also must remember, at all times, that these are real, human bodies we are addressing. And no body is perfect.

5

Mother Monster and Q.U.E.E.N.

Context Challenging and Changing
the Problematic

"Ugh, I'm so jealous that you get to write about that," my friend looked longingly at my annotated articles stacked on the coffee table, with topics ranging from Afrofuturism and *Metropolis* to queer identity in film. "I'm sitting here studying case law and you're watching that Lady Gaga video again."

I looked up from my computer, where I was, indeed, watching Lady Gaga's "Born This Way" for the tenth time that day, carefully grabbing screenshots for my paper. "I know. It's so weird. I came to Oxford to study women's issues and international politics and here I am writing about Lady Gaga. But it's important work too."

I heard a muffled snort from behind me, as one of my fellow students attempted to stifle a derisive laugh. I'm pretty accustomed to my areas of study not being seen as legitimate. When I did my first master's thesis on Harry Potter, I ended up in a long argument with a medievalist in my program about whether or not it was a legitimate area of study. And five years later, after I became a women's studies student at a research university, I've had numerous discussions justifying our presence within the academy. One of the reasons I explore the work I do, and why I'm dedicating an entire book to the work of critiquing and understanding popular culture, is because so many people engage in it. In terms of cultural understanding, there is nothing *more important* for understanding how the world works than understanding what becomes popular and why and what messages it sends. The land of celebrity is confusing and hard to navigate, but sociologists and journalists have actively created an area of cultural studies to develop these understandings. In a specific area called "fan identification," feminist scholars have picked apart and demonstrated the necessity of understanding popular culture as a social movement, particularly when queer identities intersect with popular music. How we understand our "Little Monsters" is how we understand ourselves.

Two very different figures in popular music challenge the idea that popular culture is either too problematic or too self-involved to be an area of serious study. Janelle Monáe and Lady Gaga both incorporate theory and identity into their pop work, guiding their fans into a world where pop music is a form of serious engagement with art, identity, social justice, and ideology. Both of these artists approach the project of elevating popular culture differently—and both artists have a remarkably similar ethic in their relationship to their fan base and to how they see their music as a vehicle for justice. Monáe's "Q.U.E.E.N." and Gaga's "Born This Way" are prime examples of each artist's elevation of the popular discussion. The way the music videos for each song are structured bears out these approaches to the queer identity, as Monáe plays with gendered performances that emphasize and praise differentiation, while Gaga relies on a grotesque manipulation of androgyny. Both bring theory into the mainstream, reveling in nuance and working to respond to the idea that a critic can stop at one interpretation of an idea.

As popular culture acts as a mirror for the work academics and activists do within feminism, this distinction and analysis are important for helping feminists to go deeper into our ideas of what being accountable to intersectionality truly looks like. Are we an Afrofuturist Wondaland? Or are we the children of a grotesque androgyne? And the accountability to the academic theory is an important—and currently missing—part of pop culture criticism vital to understanding the world in which we live.

A major reason that such an examination is necessary is because of the myriad ways popular artists influence and change the ways their fans respond to political discussions in the real world. Scholars Melissa Click, Hyunji Lee, and Holly Wilson Holladay explain that fan identification is the ability of a fan to see a celebrity as a friend, a hero, or a member of the same group. It thus plays a major role in how much influence that artist has outside of their musical prowess. Both Gaga and Monáe have very large fan bases that engage with their music regularly and are influenced by the political positions the artists take.

Fan identification, then, is a way in to understanding the work each artist is doing. In "Wondaland," Monáe encourages fans to use her music and her images as "freedom movements," as a form of rebellion built into the fandom. Similarly, Gaga's Little Monsters enterprise creates identification and belonging with her as a figure, creating a "surrogate voice" for those who think of themselves as outcast and voiceless.[1] Both encourage difference and lack of social conformity, but in very different ways. Monáe's "Electric Ladies" are specifically black women functioning in a white-dominated society; whereas Gaga's "Little Monsters" tend to be white, middle-class people who experience a nondominant sexual identity. The treatment of queerness within both—as a racialized and deracialized aspect of identity—is important to understanding why both fan bases come away with a differing view of their role in the political and theoretically feminist realm. These song-based symbols create a unique position for any casual consumer of popular media, as aligning oneself with one or the other has a ripple effect that moves out into the larger sociopolitical world outside of popular music. It is Nicki versus Miley, repeating itself over and over throughout the work of popular culture. This is why declaratives of persona non grata and the like are so important: we're not just dismissing a person, but also the marginalized fans of that person.

"Born This Way" was Lady Gaga's first single off her 2011 album of the same name. Critics immediately pointed out that the song aped the hook from Madonna's 1980s anthem, "Express Yourself," perhaps deliberately. Such imitation positions Gaga in the midst of a tradition of pop divas who are also queer icons. In the song itself, Gaga takes on the social message of creating a world without prejudice. Clocking in at just over seven minutes, the "Born This Way" video is a behemoth creation myth, the ultimate narrative of how "Little Monsters" came into the world and what it means to exist as one of these creatures.

In a study about the fan identification of Gaga's Little Monsters, researchers Click, Lee, and Holladay explore the ways in which Gaga's work overturns and rearticulates the idea of the "monstrous." Gaga's fans identify as outsiders, people rejected by society and often bullied. An antibullying message seems to be at the core of what Gaga's work is accomplishing, allowing young teens a safer space in which to explore and become themselves without judgment. In this way, Click and her coauthors write, Gaga becomes their voice, taking on roles the Little Monsters themselves feel less confident about. As their "mother," she is fearless—her fans see her as a figure able to take on the injustice of living as a queer person in a heteronormative and cisnormative society.

"Born This Way" opens upon a grotesque: a two-faced Mother Monster with three eyes and flowing robes restrained in gynecological stirrups, in the process of labor. As the camera—and therefore the spectator—makes eye contact with the monstrous, Gaga's introductory voiceover begins with the tale of the birth of goodness and the birth of evil, asking, "How can I protect something so perfect without evil?" We see a number of conflicting and confusing images meant to be the visualized story of the creation of the Little Monsters through this monologue. The original Mother Monster gives birth to several heads that all resemble Lady Gaga. Through a mirror-image film technique, the grotesque, messy birth is made unnerving and alarming—we see two Gagas leaning upon a faceless helper as her womb is plundered for the birth of the Little Monsters.

After the birth, the gaze travels downward, through a confused space of red and black, where naked bodies—notably, the naked bodies of black women—appear to squirm and groan in anguish. It is implied, in this imagery, and in the voiceover, that we are passing through hell. It is important to note that this is one of the few places where black bodies are fully visible without the overbearing presence of Gaga.

The birth of evil is unassisted, though Gaga is the central performer as both Mother Monster and the Mother of Evil. We see all of the Mother of Evil as she pulls a large assault rifle from her womb and begins firing, with bursts of gunfire accompanying her in a circle. This Mother is stripped down, portrayed in black and white, in contrast to Mother Monster's overwhelming use of color. As the music begins and we descend into the human world, the Mother of Evil is transposed above humanity, staring back at the viewer, asking the philosophical question: How can we protect ourselves?

The question of Gaga's song and video asks whether we can create a society in which outsiders are embraced as insiders, in which prejudice based on sexual identity or race is no more, and where it simply doesn't *matter*—as the first words of the song tell us—what your beliefs or identities are, as long as they are performed without judgment. It is looking to an overarching, happy ending, normalizing the politicized bodies of queer fans.

One of the repeating images of the video is Gaga standing with her head positioned in a line with the other monsters born of Mother Monster (who is also Gaga). All the heads resemble Gaga's own sharply shorn bob cut and dramatic makeup. Here is where Gaga's engagement with the political creates questions. Gaga's Little Monsters are not so much individualized creations of their own design, but replications—infinite and unending—of Gaga herself. Following this queen means a strange death to one's own identity in an effort to mirror her own sense of individuality. In the midst of telling us we're born this way, Gaga symbolically proclaims a conformist world in which all look like her, born of her womb, and owned by her. It is less radical ownership and autonomy and more a subculture of conformity to another dominant ideal.

It is not that people exist within their own individual identities and that these are special. Indeed, through her clumsy listing of identities, Gaga places the dominant structures on the same level as those that are traditionally oppressed. White is on the same level as black; straight is on the same level as gay or lesbian or bi. And none of it matters. The individualized queen, the patron of identity we find in Mother Monster, ultimately doesn't *care* about what makes the Little Monsters monstrous. The elevation of the political and theoretical in Gaga's creation myth is to erase societal structures.

In some ways, this is an important setting aside of that which defines us. We have the "same DNA," as the song repeats over and over. But while Gaga's anthem is focused upon queer identities, it is also shaped around whiteness—and this is important for understanding what her Little Monsters are being taught. Treasure the ways in which you're born, she says, but also be careful that you don't emphasize your race *too* much. This is about performance, darling. Gaga's casual use of colorblindness and the equating of gay and straight and bi as all the same creates a problematic ideology begging for feminist analysis.

Visually, Gaga's video seems to be about positioning herself as creator, as a deity who creates the Little Monsters. She is Mother Monster, a persona that blends with her brand. She—as a god figure—literally makes the creatures, the Little Monsters, who all are literally made in her image. While God may make no mistakes, it seems that Mother Monster has a little bit of explaining to do about why all the "different" people somehow look exactly like her. The power that this imagery and identification has to become a larger political movement is not to be ignored. The dismissal of popular culture simply because it's popular ignores the massive impact the work has on a fan base of millions. Sometimes, it's good and important to call things out as problematic, while also being aware of the good they do for their fans.

Janelle Monáe's video for "Q.U.E.E.N." offers us an alternate vision of a queen who shares the identities of her followers and incites them to rebellion. Both Gaga and Monáe's videos are remarkably similar, both opening with a monologue setting the scene for the world we're now entering. Here we are greeted by an upper-class, British, white woman, dressed professionally, in a sterile, white room. She appears on a television screen, creating distance not only from the viewer of the video, but from the tourists entering this strange museum. The woman introduces the exhibit, where we see Monáe, Erykah Badu, and the band suspended in time. These are the time-traveling rebels, the woman explains, the members of Wondaland. These rebels developed allegedly dangerous "freedom movements disguised as songs, emotion pictures, and works of art."

The mythos here is of rebellion, not creation—we are not privy to how Electric Ladies exist, but rather to the mythos of *why* they do. *The Electric Lady*—the title of Monáe's album—is a pseudonym that functions like Little Monsters, but it is less about affirming and normalizing the monstrous and more about the ownership of identity, particularly as a black female. Normalization isn't necessary. Monáe, existing within the outcast social group, appears more at ease as their notorious leader, and seems to have no problem labeling her work as rebellious.

Importantly, Monáe's work functions within the context of Afrofuturism. Afrofuturism is at once a literary technique and an ideology practiced by numerous black creatives. Ytasha L. Womack writes: "Afrofuturism is an intersection of imagination, technology, the future, and liberation."[2] For the Afrofuturist, the future of the world is a great space for imagining and realigning the universe in its moral arc toward justice. The movement—barely half a century old—imagines what a future that includes black people might look like, and does so with time-bending techniques that recall the past while looking forward to the future. Alien abduction, robots, and science fiction marvels raise questions about what it means to be human. They therefore recall the horror of slavery and what it means to be considered nonhuman or unhuman. The treatment of black bodies by Afrofuturism is at once an assertion of their humanity and a critique of their treatment as nonhuman by dominant ideologies.

Preceding *The Electric Lady*, Monáe published several works of Afrofuturistic song, reimagining the life of Maria—the female AI robot from the 1927 science fiction movie *Metropolis*—as a black slave girl android who hides in the guise of a pop star, Cindi Mayweather. *Metropolis: Suite 1* and *The ArchAndroid* lead up to *The Electric Lady*. Monáe imagines herself within an Afrofuturistic allegory, in which she is both herself and her persona as Cindi Mayweather. This shifting of identities is important to her callbacks to Electric Ladies and her specific discussions of marginalized identities within her music. Monáe is at once asserting her right to be human in a white supremacist world and playing with the idea of herself as a nonhuman subject. Tobias c. van Veen writes of the racism that creates this nonhuman positioning: "The reality of this fiction—that African-Americans are unhuman—is the constitutive paradox at work, for now it is the historical conditions themselves that are already irreal, as it were, and as they remain, wherever the 'real fiction' of racist formations take place."[3] Essentially, Afrofuturism is built out of a desire to both understand and negate the dehumanization that racism carries with it.

Thus Monáe's setting—a futuristic world in which she and her band have been imprisoned as rebellious freedom fighters—sits squarely within the traditions of Afrofuturism as it folds and bends reality and time space into an understanding of the current structures of racism and racialized violence. The video is in the future but references the past, from the African men playing the drums to the styles of music employed throughout the song, from the drum beats to the funk dance references to the use of electronica. Her stance as a leader and a black woman takes on new meaning within this Afrofuture, where her imprisonment in the museum is both an allegory for the current treatment of black people in America and a reality as she feels imprisoned by the labels pinned upon her as an artist by the media. She is a subject of suspicion, a nonhuman person suspended in time, because of the freedom she dares sing and proclaim. As van Veen notes, "Monáe, a third-generation Afrofuturist, is particularly attentive to the ways in which the android speaks to (post) modernist forms of bondage—and autonomy."

Additionally, Monáe adds a specifically feminist aspect to the world of musical Afrofuturism. Authors Daylanne English and Alvin Kim comment that Monáe "mov[es] beyond the normative feminine."[4] She relies on the elements of love, on loving oneself above all, which is seen most clearly in "Q.U.E.E.N." English and Kim continue: "With this inclusion of us, as listeners, in her narrative of politicized love and her synthesis of sounds, Monáe potentially creates an exceptionally broad and inclusive technocultural community, one that empowers androids and humans alike." Indeed, like Gaga's Little Monsters, Monáe's Electric Ladies exist on the margins of society, inhabiting both the feminine and masculine and living in a world that makes it hard for them to love themselves. Monáe sees love as the central tenet of rebellion, of breaking down those systems that create oppression. This is the kind of fan service that forces fans into a better place in the world and affirms their identities. It is what we feminists would call intersectional, and Monáe elevates her music into political movement with these steps.

Monáe's anthem is less explicitly about queerness—she does not necessarily call out specific identities by name. But lyrical referents create a space in which her black female audience knows and sees themselves, with references to chicken "wangs" and Harriet Tubman. For her fans, this explicit blackness is deeply important— she is, like Beyoncé, engaged in the insertion of blackness into a mostly white world.

Throughout her work, Monáe responds to the sexualization and animalization of black women by appearing as everything at once. Monáe's costuming and the way she comports herself is bold and delicate, fearsome and shy. She plays both ends against the middle while playing with her femininity, responding to and engaging with stereotypes that face her and her fans as black women. This represents for her fans a potent emblem of blackness, untouched and unfiltered.

But Monáe's fierceness comes at a price: "Q.U.E.E.N." also expresses the anxiety that fans might feel from sitting at the intersection of blackness and queerness. She asks over and over if she's a freak and turns the question into the hook of the song. She doesn't think being a "freak" is a bad thing, but she knows that the words the dominant society has used to cast aside people like her are hard to reclaim and hard to rearticulate well. Rather than reclaiming slurs, Monáe instead claims a dominant phrase that's rarely been allowed for people like her—"queen." Indeed, Monáe told Fuse, when the video released, that the title of the song is an acronym: Q is for Queer, U for Untouchables, E for Emigrants, the second E for the Excommunicated, and the N for "those labeled negroid."[5] "Even if it makes others uncomfortable," she proclaims, "I will love who I am." This subtle repositioning of the "freak" as a vessel for radical love bucks the system of dominance. Monáe knows she's judged. That's why she asks if God will accept her. But she realizes that it is not living without judgment that is the goal. It is standing up in the face of judgment and saying that judgment has no power over her. Monáe seems to posit heaven as a white space, one of clean lines and unflinching ideology. By existing in the transition between black and white, she is unsure if this white heaven will accept her. Perhaps, she suggests, the problem lies not with her but with the entire "program"—simultaneously programming language and a metaphor for the structure of society as a whole, again Afrofuturistic. In "Q.U.E.E.N.," religion becomes part of the structural violence—a white God unable to accept her transitional, liminal state.

And it is in this liminal state that Monáe's Electric Ladies exist. In this strange combination between human and unhuman, forever existing as a metaphor for pain and experiencing that pain themselves, Monáe's music encourages rebellion and release from these prisons. Rather than creating monstrous minions who are defined solely by their outsider status—despite having a "queen" who is every part an insider—Monáe's Electric Ladies defy categorization, united only by the desire to overturn the system. This is a freedom melody, a slave song, a path into the free world. The goal is not the radical assertion that demands LGBTQ+ people be acceptable in a heteronormative culture, but rather that we reconstitute culture altogether . . . altogether.

A much more useful hermeneutic, then, is whether or not such music and such branding and creations are *politically useful*. Here is where the argument gets truly complicated: it can be argued that Lady Gaga's bolstering of queer identities through her music inspired fans to speak up and take part in specific political campaigns. Much like Cher and Madonna before her, Gaga has become a gay icon—a beautiful white woman praised mostly by gay men for her unabashedly glamorous performances. These divas often carry political clout, creating a space for gay men to unite under a communal banner. These women become part of the language of gay culture, a method of communication and understanding between fans. In Gaga's social media–aided community, her Little Monsters are able to mobilize on her behalf. Click writes:

Through their involvement with the community built around Lady Gaga, Little Monsters have reappropriated the term "monster" by rearticulating its outsider status to inner strength and originality. No longer a negative label suggesting an inferiority to the norm, "monster" becomes, through its association with Lady Gaga, a positive point of identification for followers who wish to celebrate their differences and find strength through association with other monsters, including Lady Gaga.[6]

These Little Monsters have become a politically relevant demographic, mobilizing their communities in various ways to fight for marriage equality all over the United States. The uniting, political power of the anthem "Born This Way" cannot be denied. This is why it remains important to take popular culture seriously—Gaga has demonstrated and continues to demonstrate an immense power to influence and change political power in real time.

Monáe's politics have become more apparent even just in the past year, and she encourages her fans to think for themselves. As Alyssa Rosenberg writes in the *Washington Post*: "Her politics never fit neatly into any sort of partisan split, nor did they track directly with emerging progressive thought, and that was sort of the point."[7] In August 2015, she released "Hell You Talmbout," a song that functions as an anthem for the Black Lives Matter movement. She sings the names of the dead over a marching band beat and her voice cracks when she says the name of Sandra Bland, a woman who died in a Texas jail under suspicious circumstances. On an Instagram post about the song, Monáe became even more explicit:

> It carries the unbearable anguish of millions. We recorded it to channel the pain, fear, and trauma caused by the ongoing slaughter of our brothers and sisters. We recorded it to challenge the indifference, disregard, and negligence of all who remain quiet about this issue. Silence is our enemy. Sound is our weapon. They say a question lives forever until it gets the answer it deserves.... Won't you say their names?[8]

In a departure from her Afrofuturism here, Monáe comes back down to earth and inserts herself explicitly into a political movement she has been playing at the edges of for ages. Her Afrofuturist work has always been political, to be sure, but "Hell You Talmbout" makes her positioning explicit. All the work of queer flagging, of asserting individuality in the face of conformity, of making sure to make others uncomfortable has come to a head in this explicitly political act. And it's important that her politics here are deliberately uncomfortable for many people. She doesn't care if she makes others uncomfortable and has no interest in making sure that her monstrousness ever becomes an insider movement. She's on the margins and she's fine with that. Her Electric Ladies are changing the world outside of the neoliberal war room, and that is her place.

Both of these artists demonstrate the need to take popular culture seriously—conversations are happening that can be dissected and understood and explored. We sit in an amazing position, having access to thousands of pages of criticism and artistic transformation of that criticism and theory at the same time, all from the comfort of our living rooms. And when we wrongly use that criticism to problematize, to declare people outside of the bounds of humanity, to draw lines in the sand about what is or is not acceptable, we are failing to account for the serious ways in which this culture shapes our world even as it is problematic. Our blacklists simply fail to capture the whole of the project that is engaging with popular culture. When we dismiss, we end up unable to find ourselves in culture as well.

6

Friendly Fire

Why Our Perfectionist Lens Makes
Us Harsher on Feminist Media

When I was a kid, my brothers and I fought over who got to wear the one Superman costume my family had. There was a short period of overlap when it fit both my brothers and me—it was a little big on me, but just right on my brothers, and all of us wanted to be Superman for Halloween. During some point of the fight, I managed to get the costume on and I remember proudly marching around the neighborhood—weeks before Halloween—with the red cape flowing out behind me.

My family was into superheroes when we were growing up. We watched the TV melodrama *Lois and Clark* and went to action movies like they were going out of style. My brothers and I admired *Indiana Jones* and *Star Wars*. The release of *Star Wars: The Phantom Menace* was the most exciting moment of my middle-school years. When superhero movies came back in style, we gathered groups of our friends to go, frequently on opening weekends. I saw the first *Iron Man* movie three or four times in theaters and went to *The Dark Knight* three times over opening weekend.

But as I grew more aware of my feminist leanings, and more fully embraced a critical feminism, I realized a few key things: my heroes were all men, and all the women had really terrible backstories. In *Watchmen*, the female heroes were all victims of some kind of sexual assault. In *V for Vendetta*, the main character is tortured by V until she learns the true meaning of resistance. Jessica Jones was a rape victim. The Black Widow is an orphaned product of Soviet brainwashing. A woman without a traumatic backstory was a woman without development as a character in the comic book world.

Sexualized violence has become a method of shortening backstory—if we know that a female character was raped, we can predict certain things about the direction her character is about to take. She'll be hesitant around men. She'll have trouble connecting sexually. She'll be stunted, angry, emotionally untethered or emotionally cold, depending on which one is necessary for the plot. Numerous feminist critics have pretty much beaten this horse to death, to the point that a show featuring a rape victim as a character is almost immediately met with rolled eyes and a groan. The big revelation that's supposed to make that character make sense instead offers us a cheap shortcut to supposed character development. It's so common that the television criticism site TV Tropes developed a name for it: broken bird syndrome. The beautiful, delicate baby bird is injured in some way, and we are supposed to take pity on it and mourn the loss of its beauty and inability to fly.

The cynical eye roll is a solid and good response to most of these things—we as a culture need to step away from the desire to make women "interesting" by inflicting sexual violence on them. And as the cultural conversation about rape and rape culture has changed, we've seen a shift toward more nuanced understandings of sexual violence within our television shows.

Rape culture is a buzzword common to feminist circles over the past decade, but it's important to recognize that it's not well known outside of that particular group. Rape culture is a culture in which rape is normalized and taken as an everyday given. Comments like "boys will be boys," convicted rapists like Mike Tyson appearing as "comedy" in movies like *The Hangover*, and the normalization of Donald Trump's comment about "grab[bing women] by the pussy" in the 2016 election are all rape culture. And, naturally, popular culture frequently reinforces tropes of rape culture by turning rape into a joke, using it as a shorthand for trauma, or as a point to shock.

In the popular HBO series *Game of Thrones*, rape is almost as frequent as consensual sex scenes, used to demonstrate how barbaric particular leaders are. Perhaps the most shocking of these (many) scenes appears in season one. When Daenerys Targaryen is first married to Khal Drogo, the king of a people of horse-riders (and, notably, one of the only men of color in the series), the consummation of their marriage gets lost in the translation from book to screen. In the book, Daenerys and Drogo consummate the marriage consensually, with Drogo actually respecting the position Daenerys is in as a young woman in a foreign country, sold to the king of a foreign tribe. He checks with her, asking for consent in her language, and waits until she actively participates before making any move toward full consummation.

But on TV? He forcefully bends her over a rock, and rapes her, laying his claim upon her body. It's no mistake that one of the most lasting images from the first season of *Game of Thrones* is of a beautiful white woman being "defiled" by a man of color twice her size. Indeed, he rapes her multiple times throughout the first months of their marriage until she finally realizes she can take control and "make him happy." Pop culture conflates rape and sex in ways that blur the lines, obscuring consent.

It's the critique du jour to attack rape culture, and rightly so. Feminist critics everywhere have made incredible gains in bringing the discussion of rape and sexual assault to the forefront of the national discussion. We've surprised the makers and creators of our media, calling them directly on the carpet for their use of sexual assault as a means of character development. In 2016, Linda Holmes, NPR host and all-around badass, asked HBO's president of programming, Casey Bloys, about the network relying too heavily on sexual violence against women to drive the narrative. Bloys was caught off guard. He first called the violence on *Game of Thrones* indiscriminate and then proclaimed, "We're going to kill everybody"—which, of course, doesn't answer the question of specific sexualized violence directed at female characters.

Indeed, Bloys's joking attempt to answer a question he was utterly unprepared for indicates a deeper problem among the creatives and producers who put together all those immensely popular shows that we eat up like candy corn in October. Sexual violence is a trope that is simply taken as fact. It's a device so many have come to rely on that it's no longer significant or noteworthy to many of them. And feminist criticism has played a significant role in waking producers and writers and actors up to the fact that women's lives are not tropes, are not flat foils for male character development. We've shown ourselves to be a powerful demographic, and that power is hard to ignore.

We've begun to see intelligent discussions of rape culture from within popular culture itself, namely in the superhero series *Jessica Jones*, adapted for the screen by Netflix. The series tells the story of Jessica Jones, an ordinary woman with some extraordinary powers: extreme strength and a strange jumping ability that allows her to leap easily up buildings like a flea jumping onto a dog twelve times its height.

Jones was convinced by her best friend, Trish, to explore using her powers for good—to become a hero and help people who were hurt. In the course of attempting to do this, she runs across her eventual nemesis, Kilgrave. Kilgrave possesses powers of his own—he has the ability to make anyone in his presence do what he wants. This extraordinary ability has caused Kilgrave to maladapt into a serial murderer who uses other people's bodies for his own pleasure. He uses his powers on Jessica to force her into a relationship with him— one in which he continually uses his powers to hold her prisoner, to rape and sexually assault her, and to own her body. She spends months in therapy, growing strong enough to confront him—but still running scared when there's word of him in town. After she finally discovers an immunity to his power and escapes, she confronts her abuser, playing him until the last minute so she can get close enough to finally end him forever.

Jessica Jones is the first show I've encountered where one of the female characters has experienced trauma and it actually appears to affect her—and not just in a way that furthers the plot, but in a way that actually makes her real as a character. She has panic attacks. She needs therapy she can't afford. She's barely holding on and has developed a drinking problem. And she doesn't suddenly let go of that trauma when "duty calls" on her to be brave. She almost runs away. The portrayal of Jones's posttraumatic stress and ongoing battle against her own anxiety is accurate, well developed, and not simply a plot device.

The show itself engages with rape culture, with people protecting and dismissing Jessica's rapist in numerous ways—first by not believing her, and then by undermining her efforts to bring him to justice. Her rapist himself gaslights her, attempting to convince her that what happened wasn't rape—it was consensual, despite Jessica's protestations and his ability to control her every move.

The feminist criticism of rape culture has, in many ways, main-streamed feminist ideals. *Jessica Jones* is a show that deserves great praise because of how it manages to embrace and understand the truth of sexual violence. Feminist critique made that happen, and that's good. We should be happy. And yet, in the wake of such a popular and deeply feminist series coming out, I saw headlines and think pieces about how it wasn't enough, it wasn't there yet, we weren't yet at *perfect*. One such piece was from comedian and author Jenny Trout. After witnessing Redditors on r/fatpeoplehate gleefully manufacturing outrage over the lack of a trigger warning for one line in the show ("two minutes on the treadmill, twenty minutes on the quarter pounder"), Trout calls out her fellow feminists:

"But it's feminist here! And over here!" you might be tempted to cry. Put a hold on that transaction, because I'm not buying. If I'm willing to cop to my seasonal worship of the misogynist shit-fest that is Love, Actually, you can good and goddamn admit that your unproblematic fave has two lines that are problematic, and you can take two seconds out of your day to acknowledge that and give fat women a head's up.[1]

Perhaps Trout is right. Perhaps her fellow feminists—not all of whom are skinny women, myself included—failed in some way by refusing to note that the derisive line exists in the first episode of the show. I understand some of the offense Trout feels, knowing that it is something she has said to herself previously. But what I don't understand is the downgrading of the show from "omg I love this" to "it's okay," based on one five-second line that's not a joke, that's not actually meant for laughs. It's a line meant to show how truly fucked up Jessica Jones's life is. She stalks and judges other people, drinks herself into a stupor, and lives in her office. It landed wrong and didn't consider those who have suffered with disordered eating. I'll grant that. But what I don't get is the anger at fellow feminists for not mentioning it. Trout's critique seems to be the sort of thing written out of a desire for perfection—which is the issue plaguing modern critical feminism. The criticism—and the anger invoked— seem disproportionate to the matter at hand. One line, as folks in the comments of Trout's post said, turned a good, feminist show into something they couldn't watch.

A word before we go on, about trigger warnings and content notes: one of the major points of Trout's post is that no one warned her about that line in the show, which brought up feelings of self-hatred and disordered eating from her past. This kind of reaction is understandable, and I stand in favor of trigger warnings. What I do object to, however, is then taking that triggering content as a reason the show is a critical failure or something people should not watch. It doesn't let people make their own decisions about the show and doesn't encourage healthy critical thinking. What's more is that Trout watched the entire run and concentrates on that line, rather than the episode wherein Trish, Jessica's best friend, is forced to become bulimic at the hands of her fame-seeking mother. The concentration on one scene and not the other demonstrates how these situations that trigger a person's PTSD are deeply personal, and therefore not a solid metric for measuring the overall *critical worth* of the show.

Much of feminism, in instructing women to trust our guts, to not be gaslighted, unfortunately makes the mistake of sanctioning a person's reaction as enough to dismiss a show, rather than interrogating *why* that reaction occurred. We must engage our critical faculties with our own feelings. I don't like Kylo Ren in the new *Star Wars* films because I don't like Adam Driver because he played a rapist on another television show and made it so I couldn't personally watch the show. This does not mean his character (though whiney) is useless or a casting error. I have to interrogate my visceral reaction and separate it, in some ways, from whether or not a piece of art is saying worthwhile things.

To know exactly how skewed this conflation of personal emotional reaction and worth of media is we have to look outside of feminist popular culture, at how more mainstream shows handle sexual violence. One of the issues we have with feminist criticism is that it has a tendency to be insular, to create arguments that are inaccessible to people outside of the feminist sphere. HBO head of programming, Bloys, had no idea what the questions being asked of him were even about, because he was so unaccustomed to consuming feminist or women-led media.

The immensely popular and long-running crime procedural *Criminal Minds* uses the "rape as backstory" trope throughout the series, very often attributing different actions to sexual abuse in a person's past. The show follows the story of the Behavioral Analysis Unit (or BAU) of the FBI. These specialized agents investigate serial killers or particularly brutal murders. Their job is to get into the heads of the killer or killers and figure out how to get a few steps ahead of them.

Their cases almost always involve forms of sexualized violence. "Stabbing is a substitute for rape" is said so much in the show that by the sixth season, the characters lampshade the trope as they repeat it—calling it out as "oh, it's another stabbing. We know what that means." And yet, stabbed, brutalized, and violated female bodies litter the show like a ticker tape parade.

A raped woman takes revenge on her attackers.

A woman is raped while the husband watches.

One of the women in the squad is continually used as a prop in luring a killer into a sting, despite her own history of trauma and the very obvious effects it triggers for her.

Trauma is regular and beastly and a brutal reality of the show. There are occasional asides as to how hard the job is and how the squad has to deal with it, but on the whole, the characters see all this sexualized violence, every single day, and it largely has little effect on their lives outside of work. This is most significantly asserted in the character of Derek Morgan, a handsome, intelligent, and muscle-y African American member of the squad. In the second season, it's revealed that Morgan was the victim of childhood molestation when he's forced to confront his abuser on a trip home. It's a moving episode—and it's followed up by absolutely nothing. No "broken bird" syndrome. No ongoing trauma. Just Morgan, back to his routine of dealing with rapists and killers and the worst human nature has to offer.

It seems fairly odd that such trauma would seemingly have no effect on the agent, especially after it's all wrenched to the surface in a fairly horrifying manner. He's accused of murder and forced to reveal his past in order to catch the person he knows is the real killer—his own abuser. And then the series moves on and barely acknowledges something that would normally require therapy and a hiatus from work to deal with. It's only "special" cases that have reverberating effects within the series, and apparently the case of Derek Morgan having spent most of his childhood being repeatedly assaulted by an adult he was supposed to trust isn't special enough.

It's not special, that is, until nearly five whole seasons later, when the victim of a crime is a young boy, abducted at seven years old and kept for nearly ten years by a pedophilic sadist. It's not that they haven't encountered a case like this in intervening years—

they most certainly had. But for some reason, the writers decide to bring Morgan's past back into the picture as a means for him to connect to the mute victim of the crime. This is the only time Morgan's past is referenced, and the only time it appears to actually affect how he approaches the case (he actively assaults the criminal, an old man, before being forcibly removed from the fight). In a real-world scenario, Morgan would face disciplinary action and we'd see him being forced to meet with a therapist. But here? For a member of the BAU? Using violence to work out your own violent past is just another day.

One would hope to say *Criminal Minds* is an exception to the way our creative endeavors deal with trauma, but it's not. All too often, rape becomes just part of the backstory of a character, a fast way to develop and understand that person or to further the plot a little bit more. It's presumed, if the rape is in the past, that the person has already done the work to "get over it." If it happens on the show, that person can now develop their character in a way that tells us what kind of person they are: Are they the strong type who can just walk past trauma? Or are they "weak" and have to take a two week vacation to deal with it? Because the schedules of television and audience demand that characters never be irrevocably broken—we want of our characters what we hope is possible in real life: that those who experience sexual assault and rape can figure out ways to be strong through it, and bounce back, and not let it change who they really are on the inside. If we admit that rape has deep, lasting effects on a person that can't be solved by a two-week vacation from work, then we have to admit that we might be bad at handling sexual violence in the real world.

This is why it is so revolutionary that *Jessica Jones* refuses to present us with a woman who falls into either one of the typical categories facing victims of trauma in popular culture. She is at once weak and strong and broken and together, all at once. She hasn't lost hope in the world despite being deeply cynical. She's still functioning, forging her own way, developing her own path as a private investigator, even if she must do those things in a nontraditional manner, using her superpowers sparingly. And she still has moments where her posttraumatic stress is triggered and she has to use mechanisms taught to her by her erstwhile therapist in order to move on.

Perhaps most poignantly, though, is the moment when Jessica has the chance to confront her own abuser. She knows she has to defeat Kilgrave, and in order to do that, for a time, she must allow herself to live in the same house as Kilgrave. Indeed, she must live in her childhood home, already a scene of tragedy and memories of a family ripped from her by a tragic accident. Kilgrave is manipulating her—she knows it, and he believes his manipulation is for her own good. When she sets a boundary by telling him not to touch her, not to go near her as part of their agreement, he balks:

KILGRAVE: We used to do a lot more than just touch hands.
JESSICA: Yeah, it's called rape.
KILGRAVE: What? Which part of staying in five-star hotels, eating in all the best places, doing whatever the hell you wanted, is rape?
JESSICA: The part where I didn't wanna do any of it! Not only did you physically rape me, but you violated every cell in my body and every thought in my goddamn head.
KILGRAVE: That's not what I was trying to—
JESSICA: It doesn't matter what you were trying to do! You raped me again and again—
KILGRAVE: No—
JESSICA: —And again and again!

Kilgrave, confronted with a narrative that does not match his own version of events, that positions him as a rapist, an abuser, an enemy, begins to scream: "How was I supposed to know? Huh? I never know if someone is doing what they want or what I tell them to!"

He is beginning to turn things around to make himself the victim. And Jessica refuses him the pity that would allow him to get away with everything: "Oh poor you," she spits out sarcastically, refusing to care. It is this resistance, this conversation that is so pivotal in the series. Instead of allowing doubt, instead of allowing Kilgrave to become piteous, the "rapist with a heart of gold," *Jessica Jones* resists. It places blame squarely on the shoulders of Kilgrave, on the shoulders of the rapist who coerced sex out of his victims. And it highlights his own unwillingness to see himself as a bad person—which is central to maintaining rape culture. It's the response of the rapist that says, "I'm not bad, I'm not terrible, your memory must be faulty." And *Jessica Jones* looks at that and says no—to all of it.

Jones emphasizes for all of us the importance of addressing not only sexual violence, but the ramifications of that violence—the trauma that stems from it, and the ways in which the perpetrators of that violence resist any categorization as wrong or bad. This emphasis illustrates how rape and trauma can be handled *well*—how the various events of our lives can come together to impact every moment, and how we are not "broken" or "damaged" for dealing with that trauma. It also gives us a hero to look at who confronts her abuser, resists his gaslighting behavior, and holds her own—a way for viewers to live the experience of confrontation vicariously.

This, ultimately, is what's important about it as well. As viewers, it's important that we see our lives reflected on screen, even if they are done imperfectly—even if Jessica Jones is a drunk who is struggling to put her life together. In those few seconds when she's able to confront Kilgrave, we see a possibility of who we could be as survivors of trauma. We are affirmed that what happened was not okay, that what we know of our past is serious and understood, and that our truth is more important than what our abuser is saying. This kind of representation has power that cannot be underestimated.

And this is precisely why making the perfect the enemy of the good can be dangerous—we risk turning good media bad by our perfectionist desire for perfect characters. Art is flawed. It always will be. But feminist media has become increasingly perfectionist with the masses of access both to popular culture and basic understandings of feminist theory. Just as you should never meet your heroes, you should probably not read feminist critiques of your favorite shows if you want to keep liking them.

But perhaps that is too far. The balance has to be somewhere between blind consumption of media and angry dismissal of everything that doesn't match our extremely high standards. We all have to decide and give ourselves permission to enjoy the things that mess up and offer our enjoyment of them without qualification or accusation. We shouldn't have to constantly feel guilty about the pleasures we're taking.

When our "real-life dramas" address important feminist issues, it is often handled in incredibly clunky ways—*Criminal Minds* throwing in lines about women not reporting because the system doesn't believe them, Olivia Benson finding healing in an unbelievably quick timeline on *Law and Order: SVU*. The ways in which popular culture reflects our conversations about sexual trauma indicates that something is broken about how our culture comports itself, and that is the conversation *Jessica Jones* addresses.

The truth of the matter is that the creators of film and television stories often don't know how to write women—at least not well. They are either imbued with some kind of extra super power, mistake fist-fighting for strength, or are irreparably damaged and in need of rescue. Often, they are all three. It is this treatment of women that makes it impossibly hard to discuss sexual violence in meaningful and accurate ways. In order to maintain a relationship with a cultural conversation about rape that is progressing very fast, we must also ensure that our popular culture reflects these conversations accurately.

So how can we encourage and develop an awareness for how women are understood in our popular culture, particularly in the serious discussions and television shows we praise, while understanding that progress is not going to happen overnight?

We read women. We employ women. We listen to women. It's really as simple as that. The way to create *real* women on the screen, rather than facsimiles, is to have more women involved in the production and in the business. The fact of the matter is that the discourse will not change until we recognize that women actually have important things to contribute, not only to criticism but to art itself. It is not so strange that a woman is able to more accurately portray the inner life of a woman than a man who has no experience living as a woman does. These conversations won't be productive or efficient without women being centered in them.

This is the only way forward. It's not radical. It's not revolutionary. It's not burning the whole system down. But it is what works. We've seen a greater feminist awareness in our media overall because we've seen more and more minority genders involved in the creation of these television programs. Putting more women in charge has given us *Scandal*, *Grey's Anatomy*, and *How to Get Away with Murder*. Putting more women in charge has given us a Wonder Woman movie and a revitalization of comics focused on and featuring female superheroes. More women involved have given us *Sense8*, *Broad City*, and *Jane the Virgin*. Women-helmed TV gave us *Orange Is the New Black*.

The chances for greater creativity, representation, and uniquely important storytelling that don't shove women into one typecast box are increased when women are involved on all levels. Our art becomes *better*—better at telling our own stories, better at representing us, better at simply being art. This doesn't mean this art should be free from critique—it just means that we're still in a learning stage where it is more important that we have a diversity of women on TV available for critique. We're still grasping for representation, and we need to acknowledge those steps toward it, even if some of those portrayals don't quite work. We're already seeing important transitions away from tropes about sexual violence, as *Jessica Jones* demonstrates. Now we just need to move toward further diversity of those experiences.

7

Actually, It's about Ethics in Feminist Criticism

Where White Feminism and #GamerGate Converge

"We don't think the internet is real," feminist critic and firebrand Anita Sarkeesian told the Daily Beast in 2016. "We still don't. And when it comes to harassment we all internalize this message, this sticks and stones kind of thing, which I think is bullshit. Because it *is* trauma and we are being *traumatized*. It's hard to believe that things that people say online can hurt us and affect us that much or impact our daily lives, but they do."[1]

In 2014 Sarkeesian ended up at the center of a perfect storm of misogyny, hatred, and harassment. When she attempted to raise money to fund a YouTube project performing critical feminist analysis of video games, a subset of the gaming community, composed mainly of white men, struck back, hard. Sarkeesian faced violent harassment daily, with someone even creating an app where the user gained points the more you beat up a facsimile of Sarkeesian's face.

But Sarkeesian's harassment wasn't isolated. It was part and parcel of a larger movement that would be collectively known as #GamerGate.

#GamerGate was born out of a relationship gone sour. When indie game designer Zoë Quinn broke up with her now ex-boyfriend Eron Gjoni, she had no idea how much rage one man could have. Quinn had published a text-based, role-playing game called *Depression*

Quest in 2013, around the same time she was dating Gjoni. After they broke up in 2014, Gjoni wrote several inflammatory blog posts alleging that Quinn had (1) cheated on him, and (2) slept with gaming journalists as a means of securing positive press for her game. The posts hit a nerve, particularly with a community of men whose identity is wrapped up in their knowledge of games and their own taste in what they think makes a good game.

Zoë's attempts to break into this male-dominated sphere were already tough, but to now have the weight of a misogynist ex accusing her of sleeping her way to good reviews for her games made her life hell. She, like Sarkeesian, faced harassment daily and was even forced to temporarily move out of her home due to threats against her life. For more than a year, #GamerGate dominated the conversation about criticism in the video game world. It brought forth an absolutely chilling effect on the world of criticism, removing one of the few tools feminists have at our disposal to attempt to make the culture that we live in better.

#GamerGate is not necessarily unique in the world of criticism. To the contrary, misogyny isn't confined to gamers and it's not just the purview of the nerds. The election of Donald Trump, the rise of right-wing, anti-Progressive political movements across the Western world tell us it's not. The need for focused, independent feminist criticism is important to a healthy cultural exchange of ideas—and it must be free of harassment. And that means feminist criticism *itself* must pay close attention to lessons we can learn from #GamerGate.

A postmortem analysis of #GamerGate is important for understanding just how ideological purity, hatred of personality, and identity wrapped up in a movement can become deeply concerning. It highlights a number of warning signs for our outsized sense of our own importance in critical thought.

Much of #GamerGate's controversy was a clash between the old guard and a progressive, diverse, critical faction. There have been women involved in gaming since computers were a thing, but somewhere along the way, gaming companies and marketers decided that appealing to a large demographic of white men under thirty-five was the way to go to make money. This focus created an insular demographic—video gaming was "uncool," and being a gamer was considered a negative aspect of a person's personality. Popular culture placed the "nerd" as an unwanted social outcast, a loser who spent more time playing Tekken than doing anything else. So the "gamer" identity was developed as a way to defend themselves. Gaming takes skill and hard work and dedication, and gamers took these positive aspects and built a multibillion-dollar industry around it.

In response to a cultural stereotype of video gamers as nerdy, geeky, slothful virgins, gamers developed a strictly policed community of people who fit into a very specific identity. People who dedicated their lives to gaming, who saw games as the true form of art, and who knew how to analyze the art of it all became markers of the gamer identity. A true gamer knows every little detail—or, at least, that's the test gamers give to people they suspect are not "real" gamers. The gamer identity became about obsessively memorizing every tiny fact in order to prove one's worthiness for the throne.

Much of the gamer identity is also built upon rejection from mainstream society. A very specific mythos and ideals about why and how a person has trouble with relationships are explained through the gamer identity: "I am rejected because I am a nerd, and society doesn't understand me." This mythos becomes a self-segregating, self-fulfilling prophecy—as the gamer lives up to the markers of the gamer identity, they begin to separate themselves from "the normals," therefore appearing to be persecuted by society. They are rejecting before they are rejected, in other words, and blaming those they reject.

This pathos is, of course, not the entirety of a vast and diverse gaming community, but it is indicative of a subset of that community that wraps their identity within their hobby. These are the true believers—the only ones who "get it," who know these games inside and out. Because they are an economic force within the industry and their outsider status has been confirmed for them in marketing, they develop an outsized sense of their power within the larger entertainment community. And they aggressively force others who claim their label to be on the same side—a concept called "forced teaming." Forced teaming is an abuse tactic aimed at creating a sense of togetherness because of a shared circumstance or identifying label. So if you're really a feminist, you'll believe X, Y, and Z. If you're really a gamer, you'll defend gaming culture with us.

This forced teaming happens when members of a community centered on a particular identity are coerced into a relationship where trust has not yet been earned. These communities that form around the shared identity need time to develop and be understood, and the emotional push for relationship based solely on shared identity disallows a slow, trust-building process. I certainly get along better with friends who "get it"—who understand what being a bisexual feminist in the Midwest is like and to whom I can speak with about these issues. The dangerous part is when that identity serves as shorthand for a group, for an entire set of assumed values the group believes in. We assume that if someone identifies as "gamer" that they can then be trusted to behave in specific ways, because of this forced teaming dynamic. When the person fails to live up to unwritten, unspoken expectation, they are browbeaten into conformity or ousted from the group entirely.

And again, while this applies to a subset of the feminist community, it needs to be excised like a cancerous tumor because it has the ability to affect any and all feminist discourse. The mainstreaming of this kind of thought will affect how feminists work and enact their activism in the future. We see it most clearly in white feminist responses to callouts on racist behavior or issues. The "Black Twitter is mean to me" tears of the white feminist are a major part of the identitarian political force within mainstream white feminism. The idea that representatives of Black Twitter are not following the rules of white feminism—the required levels of politeness, the conception that talking about race is racist, and those unspoken "you don't challenge this person" rules—is an emulsifying force among white feminists. By lumping legitimate criticism in with harassment, because it doesn't follow the rules of the dominant group, white feminism reinforces racial politics that have plagued feminism for centuries. And they force other feminists to team up with them in enforcing the perceived identity of the group label.

This forced teaming happens so quickly and so easily that many don't realize they're part of it. For example, when the biggest protest in U.S. history—the Women's March on Washington—took place, there was a lot of hubbub about the leadership of the march rejecting pro-life groups who attempted to partner. The magazine *Christianity Today* published a long op-ed that was essentially an exercise in forced teaming: if you want to march and be totally intersectional, you have to include Christian voices (which the writer then force-teamed into also being pro-life). In order to be feminists, we *have* to be inclusive and automatically trusting of anyone who wants to support us, even if they disagree with fundamental principles of a particular movement! The big tent cannot have walls!

But the big tent does have walls, and it's perfectly okay for feminists to reject people who vote for anti-choice politicians and support organizations that work to strip people of their rights to their own body. But you wouldn't know it to hear these Christian feminists talk about it—the entire argument devolves into an exercise in forced teaming: feminists are supposed to be X, so in order for a feminist to call themselves feminist, they must follow these particular lines *I* believe of X.

Another warning sign is the perception that the identity group is working for a cause of righteousness and is therefore absolutely and always correct. Gamers within the #GamerGate movement became a mockery of themselves because they *insisted* that their cause was "about ethics in gaming journalism." A campaign of harassment targeted at women (particularly women of color) was justified in the minds of many because it wasn't about these women specifically but about the bigger ideas and ideals of corruption and ethical problems. These women just happen to be the lightning rods for all the rage and energy about poor ethics exhibited by video game journalists.

In order to understand this particular argument, we have to go back to Zoë Quinn. One of the reasons her ex-boyfriend's missives took on such force is because he tied them into a perceived problem with gaming reviews—namely, that they tend to favor games the reviewers like. This sense of righteousness requires both a lack of understanding of the issue at hand and a sense of helplessness within the larger system to change anything. Power comes from being able to control one's environment and one's position within it; and a gaming culture that's suddenly open to people who haven't "suffered" from being the nerd feels like an affront. This develops into a rage that lashes out in harassment and attempts to reinforce a point of view without listening to any other arguments. A person this deep into an identity-fueled sense of righteousness, in fact, becomes beyond persuasion.

The gamer identity, sense of marginalization, and a heaping dollop of "this person is the enemy" created the harassment campaign of #GamerGate. Under the acceptable banner of correcting ethical misdeeds and holding people accountable, the movement identified its enemies and went after them. And once someone is deemed to be outside the movement or critical of it—and therefore an enemy—the only strategy from there on out is survival: survival of the inevitable doxxing (publishing of personal information online), the harassment, the threats, and daily Twitter messages accusing you and your family of all sorts of evil misdeeds.

Similarly, the white feminist identity seems like it's about the larger issues—the desire to unite against the common enemy of sexism, the wish to make feminism translatable for the larger population, and the need to appear unimpeachable. But what it results in is anyone not toeing the white feminist line being pushed out of feminism altogether. Play nice or you'll be labeled a harasser, part of the problem, and sexist. We see this most clearly in handwringing about "callout culture" within liberal-leftist movements. The line between calling out and harassment is a thin one, especially in a world of social media "pile ons" and blacklisting that make some writers kryptonite to editors and publications. White feminism uses this handwringing to its advantage, calling for perceived harassers to be quiet, to use their voices to promote a very specific, sanitized flavor of feminism, rather than a complex, intersectional, justice-oriented feminism.

Mikki Kendall, a comic-book author and frequent fixture of Black Twitter, has been at the center of a number of these spectacular disasters of white women feeling "attacked" and using their position of privilege to attempt to silence her. Kendall has started several important hashtags and movements that call out the complicity of white women within the larger system. Her most famous is probably #solidarityisforwhitewomen, in which black women chronicled the failed work of white feminists in saying "we're all women" in response to specifically racist attacks or attacks on womankind. White feminists didn't take very kindly to it.

The sanctimonious responses of white feminists to Kendall's campaigns frequently come in the form of think pieces about harassment, frequently citing examples of black feminists harassing white women as evidence of the "toxicity" of "Twitter feminism." In a piece for *The Nation*, Michelle Goldberg attempted to find that line between harassment and critique, but it went off the rails, around the third paragraph, when she referred to feminist critique online as "some sort of Maoist hazing."[2] The stories and think pieces like Goldberg's pushed to identify white women as the victims and black feminists as the perpetrators of violence.

There's an extensive history behind this call from white women for their whiteness to protect them from minority criticism. Cultural and personal memory makes it very fraught when a white feminist is claiming to be "harassed" by a person of color, including another woman. White women—like yours truly—must be extra careful when determining what criticism we decide to label as "toxic," because that can easily fall into racial histories that devalue the work of women of color in favor of protecting the sensibility of the white woman.

When we move to discuss "toxicity" in online spaces, we must be ever cognizant of the role that the tears of white women have played in the oppression of women of color in the past. These racist attitudes toward people of color have played themselves out in mainstream feminism as well, all the way from the radical movements of the 1960s to the Slut Walks of today. There's a distinct privileging of the white feminist voice over and above the voices of women of color, and that privileging, itself, contributes to the state of feminist criticism today. We can't talk about the nuanced "problematic" areas of modern feminism without addressing, again, the continued rifts between black and white, between gay and straight and bi, between trans and cis. Feminism, as a movement, is not immune from the same methods of oppression that plague mainstream society.

One of the ways in which we've enacted this oppression is through our continued focus on making "perfect" feminism— feminism that fits a specific vision of artistic expression, a specific ideal of what feminism is or should be, a feminism developed by and for elite individuals rather than the actual consumers of popular culture.

What we have is #GamerGate Feminism, except it's not about ethics in gaming journalism, it's about what's "problematic" for feminism this week.

Let's run down the checklist: an identity-driven movement, convinced of its righteousness, hell-bent on destroying the "enemy" at all costs, and defining who that enemy is with specific in or out language determined by a sense of being "better" than everyone else.

This is both #GamerGate and mainstream, culture-critical feminism. So do feminists within this particular subset use their perceived power as a method to harass and shame other feminists?

Actually, It's about Ethics in Feminist Criticism 85

The answer is absolutely yes. The harassment is not as virulent, not "call the police and move house" bad—most of the time—but the harassment is there. People afraid to tweet. Writers afraid to publish. Speakers afraid to speak. Not because of misogynistic twitter harassers trying to doxx us—though that's a real fear—but because our own fellow feminists have created an environment in which it is impossible to have a nuanced discussion about cultural issues. One poorly phrased tweet, one misstep, can become a storm from which there is no recovery. You will forever have the scarlet letter following you. Even as feminists online don't like to think of themselves as harassers, there is a potent faction of perfectionist feminists who believe that harassment is the way forward in defense of feminism. Threats, doxxing, the siccing of bad groups upon a person. These things do happen in the name of feminism, because it is so easy to draw the line between enemy and defender—especially in a world of perfection. Because the personal is political, our individual choices within the capitalistic market are political decisions. But to hold the individual responsible for choosing to engage with the culture in a different manner is to quash the necessary dissent and discussion that is important for growth as a movement.

Increasingly, however, online feminism in particular has become a hornet's nest of blocking, muting, trolling, and subtweeting, with each person attempting to build their own little circle of sympathetic friends who will listen to them. Liking a particular celebrity or a particular song is grounds for being persona non grata in some circles—or, worse, deemed "problematic," with that label following you like a tiny cat who simply won't leave.

Take the situation of Ani DiFranco. DiFranco is a popular feminist singer who had her heyday in the late 1990s with songs like "Not a Pretty Girl" and "Untouchable Face." In 2013 she announced a retreat for feminist singers and writers in Louisiana—at Nottoway Plantation and Resort. The former plantation has been converted into a large resort hotel and, in order to market themselves better, had sanitized the fact that the plantation had once been home to hundreds of slaves. The online outrage generated because DiFranco would choose to hold a retreat at a place that represents so much pain for the black community led to the cancellation of the event. DiFranco apologized in a blog post, writing that she had initially imagined that the setting and its history might provoke some creative energy and discussions about the need for reform in the face of injustice.

The firestorm was so significant and the flame so bright that to mention DiFranco without acknowledging the problem of the plantation incident is to be seen as whitewashing her complicity in racism. Her mistake is appended to her name like a title: Ani DiFranco, Racist White Feminist. When I conducted a brief, unscientific survey on Twitter about what people think of when they hear of Ani DiFranco, "plantation racism" was the most common reply, followed by "white lady who wore dreads." Both are markers enough to deem her as an irredeemable racist, incapable of learning or moving on.

DiFranco is probably not crying into her coffee every morning about this new amendment to her biography. But, as Jon Ronson points out in *So You've Been Publicly Shamed*, these kinds of public shaming are not restricted simply to celebrities who screw up.[3] The most virulent ongoing harassment and public shaming seem targeted at ordinary citizens without a platform, those teenagers who screw up or the random feminist stepping out of line. An antifeminist point of view or mistake can be corrected. An antifeminist, as a person, cannot. I'm not going to make any headway with a virulent misogynist who believes God tells him that women are to submit to their husbands. I applaud the people who try, but there is a point at which the views *do* define the person. And it's okay for us to append that kind of thinking onto a person's biography, as it has become part of the person's sense of identity and biography by then.

Where I *am* going to make headway is with the people who have simply done a poor job of expressing a view or have made a bad choice but have otherwise shown an openness toward changing their perspective. This goes on a case-by-case basis: it took a lot of conversation with my mother to move her around to a position of affirmation of LGBT identity. It took many conversations with my friends from college to get them to understand why "men should be the heads of the house" was a bad teaching. It took a lot of work and a lot of conversation with my brother and his wife to get them around to an understanding of feminism that wasn't negative. Progress takes rebellion and protest and resistance and conversation and nuance and discussion. It takes all these different roles; and different people in them.

But what it doesn't take is the placement of a person's mistake into isolation, without regard to the rest of their character or their previous positions. There are strains of current feminism that actually advocate that we don't look at a person's history when considering whether or not a certain action is a problem—and to an extent I agree with them. People who screw up often turn to their history as an activist or some kind of advocate to clarify that they are "the least racist person ever" or some other kind of false declarative. Preventing that defense is important, but our current strategy of saying, "None of that matters, you're anti-feminist *now*," is uncharitable and stops any and all conversation. What needs to happen, instead, is a conversation along the lines of "Sure, I'll grant you that you fucked up this one time. What are you going to do to make it right?" And one hopes the person who made the error shows good faith efforts to correct themselves. If we are unwilling or unable to develop this nuance and empathy, we risk becoming as negative and irrelevant as the gamers who are still pouncing on anyone who tweets #GamerGate four years after the fact.

Unfortunately, these important, life-changing conversations are frequently lost in the noise of the internet firestorm that develops any time someone publicly fucks up. The moments after a mistake are the most crucial—an entire crowd will be watching to make sure a person apologizes correctly. And for many, the mistake has already tainted our vision of the person, moving them ever closer into that distinctive and harmful "enemies" camp. We saw this happen with #GamerGate, where journalists and companies perceived as sympathetic to the victims of #GamerGate were immediately thrown in with the enemies of the movement. They were corrupt, indefensible, and terrible people. They deserved the harassment they got. This is the new McCarthyism, the lists of personae non gratae.

Immediately following my announcement that I would be joining the Clinton campaign in Iowa in the summer of 2016, I was sent a semi-anonymous message on Tumblr asking how I, as a feminist, could possibly support a hawkish liberal like Clinton who kills small children in other countries. Because I had taken a job (that I needed) to work for a campaign for the person who many agreed had the best chance to succeed in the coming election, I was immediately tagged as a neoliberal racist, someone who supported every single bad policy that Clinton had supported and was robotically following her every whim. For this person, my decision was nothing but malice, and I had become a terrible person. I could feel the permanent mark of "worked for the Clinton campaign" spreading across my biography, like watercolor across a paper towel, developing my own unfortunate appendix of perceived errors and mistakes that made me unfeminist or possibly even antifeminist. No nuance was allowed for my personal views or motivation—I am tarred, forever, as the defender of foreign policy that results in death.

I was lucky to avoid harassment, and I shut down objections by reminding people that, hey, human being here. But the attempts to come at me were vanishingly tiny compared to the large-scale calling out that happens when someone of much higher visibility screws up. That mistake tarnishes the reputation forever, creates an environment in which the person cannot get away from attacks, and where people who don't even know the person become involved in the fray. In the wake of the Women's March, for example, a white woman tweeted a very ignorant question at a prominent figure in feminist twitter. The tweet went viral and the woman—who only had something like four hundred followers—was met with thousands of tweets flooding her timeline about how ignorant and stupid her tweet was. That woman's feminist credentials have been killed well before they even developed. It becomes part of the introduction in explaining internet drama: "She wrote about thing X and it was racist." And as a lot of feminists are fond of saying when politicians delete tweets: The Internet Is Forever.

Or it is as long as people actively work to keep the memory of errors and missteps alive.

That's the last, and most crucial, lesson of #GamerGate: it's unsustainable. The fear and anger die out eventually. Sure, some hardcore believers will always remain, always stick around, but eventually, disagreements will cause the movement to fracture and fall apart. A movement has to achieve the validation of some kind of victory in order to be sustained, and #GamerGate didn't do that—mainly because their goals were impossible. Sure, we had a "discussion" about the ethics in gaming journalism. It was that the ethics are doing just fine and why in the fuck are you telling women to go kill themselves if ethics are your goal? A movement simply aimed at some perfection where the goal posts are constantly moving? That's unsustainable.

The very loud subset of feminism that is attempting to mainstream exile others as a viable organizational practice will fall in on itself because perfection is unachievable. One of our own will screw up. One of them will screw up big. And we'll realize that the grace we afford ourselves when we screw up might—just might—be worth extending to those we've deemed as foes too.

Indeed, when Chimamanda Adichie screwed up in 2017, it was as though the feminist community went through immense and immediate whiplash. Adichie, in an interview in March 2017, commented that transgender women are fundamentally different from cisgender women in how they experience the world. Specifically, she pointed out that being perceived as male for a portion of life accords some transgender women privileges inaccessible to cisgender women. For many, this commentary read as Adichie affirming the idea that transgender women are not "real" women because they don't experience oppression in the same way as a cisgender woman who was assigned female at birth. Adichie's point lacked a certain nuance that is relevant to the debate: the idea that transgender women *do* experience a unique form of oppression due to their position in a cisnormative world that reinforces the gender binary at every turn. But her failure to distinctly lay out these ideas (and her failure to simply respond "yes" when asked if trans women are women) led many to be extremely disappointed in a feminist hero.[4] For many, she was suddenly no longer allowed in the feminist club, and her failure in nuancing a discussion of gender led some to lump her in with gender abolitionists who harass and bully transgender women. It was as though feminism as a movement could not pause and ask her to clarify further.

Our current methods of criticism—which insist on perfection over and above any other good—are infecting how we deal with actual, human people. They are creating a toxic environment where dissent is frightening and art must be carefully regulated to follow specific norms. Adichie commented soon after the trans-fail debacle that the immense amount of backlash made discussion about the subject impossible for her. Once again, we see that this kind of rubric and framework for approaching the world is simply unsustainable.

Call me unfeminist, but there has to be another way.

8

Do You Even Lift, Bro?

Toxic Masculinity, Sports Culture, and
Feminist Ignorance of the Problems

When I lived in Oxford, my room was in student housing on the north end of town. It was a weird square dormitory with an open courtyard in the middle, and a common room with a TV and various video games up on the fourth level of one side. My room was on the opposite side of the building from the common room, and any decision to go up there essentially meant a commitment to walking up and down five flights of stairs if I forgot something or had to go use the toilet. Since the room couldn't be reserved, I'd have to hope that no one was up there when I wanted to go play a video game to relax or watch some shitty television.

During certain parts of the year, I just knew it wasn't going to work: the Rugby World Cup was on, or the Euro Cup was on, or some other major sporting event would mean the room would be taken over by those tough, sporty boys who assumed I had zero interest in sports.

I have made numerous attempts to become involved in sports over the years. I've always had a passing interest in soccer, and I enjoy watching and attending games. I watch the Olympics, when I get a chance, and have favorite sports that I try to catch when they're on. I can understand and explain the offside rule in soccer and can name major players and where they're from. But, in many ways, the fans have pushed me away from the sport, making it impossible for me to enjoy it, depending on who is watching it with me.

When the Euro Cup rolled around, I tried to join a group of guys for watching a few of the games. I was immersed in dissertation work and didn't necessarily devote a lot of time or energy to keeping up with the matches—you could, accurately, call me a casual fan. And to these boys with whom I tried to watch the games, being a casual fan was an annoyance. I had to be tested, and having been found wanting, I was not worthy of sitting with them, despite the fact that I made no noise and sat out of the way. My mere presence in the room was apparently enough to make them uncomfortable.

I'd call this an anomaly, but my numerous encounters with sports-centric men have taught me that this treatment is the rule rather than the exception. If I don't have the appropriate "expert" knowledge, I'm not someone who should be joining in on sport fandom. I need to practically pass a test before I'm deemed worthy—and I've found that this test is harder in many ways simply because I'm a woman.

Sports culture is unique in the world of feminist criticism, in that it seems to be the only area that is written off solely because it's mainly such a culture of macho-centered bragging. Feminist criticism of sport tends to fall into a couple of very narrow camps: criticism of lack of equal access to all genders, or critique of sexual assault and rape culture as normalized within sports culture.

One of the primary voices in this ongoing discussion about sports culture—and one of the best feminist critics we have today—is Jessica Luther, who has been a Twitter-friend of mine for over half a decade now. Her work (partnered with fellow Texas writer Dan Solomon) has done an extraordinary job of highlighting the ways in which sports uniquely protects rapists and sexual assaulters and creates a culture so focused on winning that victims are revictimized again and again. Feminism pays deep attention to these kinds of revelations and critiques because they are part and parcel of the feminist cause—supporting victims of sexual assault who are undermined in the national media because they are accusing that sacred cow of American culture.

Luther's breakthrough article, "Silence at Baylor," went through in painstaking detail how Baylor University had failed to address a case of sexual assault committed by a football player and how the Title IX office had failed to adequately address student complaints. Other students and graduates at the university soon spoke up to corroborate the findings, and soon it was revealed that this case is the rule, not the exception. Baylor had to act. They were embroiled in national headlines for much of the next year, finally culminating in the resignation of President Kenneth Starr and the firing of head coach Art Briles.[1] In an article five months after Briles's firing, *Sports Illustrated*'s Jason Kirk explained that Briles had been fired because a violent incident had been reported to him and he did nothing.

Baylor is not alone in becoming the center of sexual assault stories surrounding male sports programs. Indeed, Luther has been a pioneering researcher in the subject, having published *Unsportsmanlike Conduct* in the fall of 2016, detailing the ways in which the admiration of football culture and rape culture mesh, and the (as of this writing, forthcoming) *How to Love Sports When They Don't Love You Back*. Her work is creating a feminist space in that world where feminist thought has traditionally followed either a line of equality (Title IX) or of dismissal. Her work is a prime example of engaging with something problematic without dismissal, without throwing the baby out with the bathwater.

And yet feminist criticism of sports is often so superficial as to step right into the "all or nothing" problem that arises in numerous cultural artifacts. Our tolerance level for shenanigans in sports suffers from an unwillingness to go any deeper into issues of toxic masculinity and how that culture insulates itself from outside criticism. It seems that our lack of critical engagement and thought is harming us most in sports, where our dismissal because of problematic elements prevents us from a very real dialogue on the effects of unchecked masculinity. Because masculinity is at once a necessary object of criticism and a barrier to becoming further involved in sport, it becomes extremely tricky to analyze as an element of sports culture: we cannot be allowed into the sports fan club if we object to the ways masculinity acts itself out because we are, ironically, not masculine ourselves. Feminism has, by and large, accepted this barrier for what it is, declaring the culture as a whole problematic and not worth our time, when we could mine so much more critical thought by getting past our self-selected barriers around sport.

In other words, while we don't need to throw the book at sports culture from a feminist perspective, we do need to broaden our criticism and understand that our dismissals of such culture help to reinforce those toxic assets that mark it as problematic. The rejection of sports by feminists (who are mostly women) reinforces that sports exist to preserve masculinity—which in turn ends up preserving the most toxic portions of that masculinity.

One of the best examples of how the rejection of female fan presence in sport, both by feminists and by sports culture, is in the reaction to the trial of O.J. Simpson in the mid-1990s. I was around ten at the time, and my parents kept me away from coverage of the case as much as they could because they considered it inappropriate. The only thing I personally remember of the time is my elementary school principal coming on the PA system during lunch, announcing the verdict. Many of the kids in my nearly all-white school cried out, shouting, "Not guilty!? But he did it! What?!" I had no idea who O.J. Simpson was or why I should care. That he was a sports figure never entered my mind because I was uninvolved in sports altogether.

But I learned later just what that case meant for the country. Simpson was a massively important football star. He was a black athlete who had *made it*: he'd won the Heisman in college. He'd played pro. He'd gotten out of the projects. He was a *star*. And he married a white woman, had a tumultuous relationship that ended in divorce, but continued to have a relationship with his ex-wife. In June 1994, his ex-wife was murdered on the front steps of her home, and a waiter from a nearby restaurant was found nearby, also dead. When police went over to O.J. Simpson's house to inform him of the death, they found Nicole's blood on his car, and a bloody glove in a pathway near the guesthouse where Simpson's friend Kato Kaelin lived.

In what was deemed the Trial of the Century by the press, the high-profile case played heavily on media optics, with O.J.'s defense team frequently using the media to create doubt about his guilt. Cameras were allowed in the courtroom, and the trial was broadcast live around the country. Media reports—and judgments—about various players in the trial became sensations, with the fashion sense of the female prosecutor becoming a major focus at different points. Responses to the trial were widely divided along racial lines: because of existing problems with police brutality and mistrust of the police in the black community, many black people thought Simpson was not guilty. White people, on the whole, believed he was guilty. The murder occurred just two years after the famous Rodney King riots, and many involved in the trial were intensely aware of how having video evidence of police brutality had forever changed the narrative. O.J.'s fame as a sports star affected how police officers and potential jurors saw him, and the case (and the eventual acquittal) is credited with starting a trend of celebrities being able to literally get away with murder because of their celebrity status—particularly sports celebrities.

One of the major problems in the case, too, was the decision by the state to assign the case to a female prosecutor, who was frequently characterized in the media as the un-woman, the woman who wasn't feminine enough, who was masculine in her presentation, and, alongside the virile masculinity of O.J., looked weak. The dynamics of a "weak" white woman going after a man's man, the Juice, also deeply influenced the trial, as the prosecutor worked to overcome not only the sexism of the court system but the sexism of the media. These lines drawn by the O.J. trial helped cement modern images of the masculine sports star—especially his abuse and control of his relationships with women. Accounts are that Simpson was extremely jealous and controlling of his ex's relationships, and that the night of the murders may have happened because of Simpson finding another man at his ex's place.

But toxic masculinity hasn't abated since it was highlighted in the days of Simpson. Indeed, the preservation of the masculinity of sports stars has marched on and on, revealed in contemporary times as a culture concomitant with sexual assault of women. To speak of specifics here is to think immediately of the national outrage that was the case of Brock Turner, a student athlete at Stanford and convicted rapist. During the first month of school, as a freshman on scholarship at Stanford, Turner was at a party and assaulted a drunken woman behind a dumpster by the side of the house. She was black-out drunk and could only fill in details of what actually happened to her through eyewitness accounts and flashes of memory from that night. What she remembers clearly is waking up in a hospital bed in a hallway, with pine needles and dirt in her hair. In a statement to the court, she wrote:

The next thing I remember I was in a gurney in a hallway. I had dried blood and bandages on the backs of my hands and elbow. I thought maybe I had fallen and was in an admin office on campus. I was very calm and wondering where my sister was. A deputy explained I had been assaulted. I still remained calm, assured he was speaking to the wrong person. I knew no one at this party. When I was finally allowed to use the restroom, I pulled down the hospital pants they had given me, went to pull down my underwear, and felt nothing. I still remember the feeling of my hands touching my skin and grabbing nothing. I looked down and there was nothing. The thin piece of fabric, the only thing between my vagina and anything else, was missing and everything inside me was silenced. I still don't have words for that feeling. In order to keep breathing, I thought maybe the policemen used scissors to cut them off for evidence.[2]

Turner's victim, a then twenty-two-year-old college graduate who had attended the party with her sister, could remember nothing of the assault. Turner was caught mid-rape by two graduate students from Sweden who happened to be biking back home from the library. One Swede chased down Turner as he ran from the scene while the other stayed with the victim and called the police. There could not be a more open-and-shut case concerning assault—the rapist was caught in the act, his victim was in and out of consciousness and was completely incoherent when she was conscious, and he ran from the scene when he was interrupted (which, if it was consensual, likely wouldn't have happened).

Nevertheless, this case of the student athlete accused of rape raised contentious debate in the national scene. Turner was, in fact, found guilty, and sentenced to just six months in jail—an absurdly light sentence for a violent sexual assault. Turner's statements since the conclusion of the case have been centered on the "dangers of alcohol." In Turner's eyes, and, as it became clear during the trial, in the eyes of many fans, Turner's athletic prowess was a tragic story ruined by underage drinking. The only way it was his fault was that he succumbed to the pressure to drink. Stanford, for its part, decided that banning hard liquor at campus parties would solve their rape issue.

But one of the major issues facing universities dealing with a toxic masculinity centered on the use and abuse of women is the fact that sports bring in millions of dollars to universities every year. College athletes are the single biggest money earners for tons of Big 12 universities, making it in the university's best interest to look the other way when the toxic masculinity of sports culture results in students who attack women.

There's a lot of masculine energy and protection of masculinity that swirls around sports culture. Watching Sunday football with a beer in hand is considered a manly right. Kate Fagan, writing for ESPNWin 2013, observed: "In sports, especially in the NFL, being a man—a man's man, a real man, a manly man—all too often means projecting an air of invincibility, a willingness to absorb pain at all costs, an expectation that even the most vicious insults can do no harm. Vulnerability is seen as weakness."[3]

Much of this masculine culture ties into a homophobic rape culture that develops somewhat uniquely within sports, thanks to the concentration of young men in an intense, high-energy activity that requires an immense need to bond with teammates. In 2004 Karen Franklin published a case study of group violence within a sporting environment, examining a case of hazing at a high school football camp in which several older male students attacked younger ones in a homophobic attack. At one point, they shoved broom handles into the rectums of their victims.

Franklin writes that this kind of violence is tied both to heterosexuality and to masculine identity, and that the violence that occurs is often the result of attempts by the group to prove masculinity to each other. Franklin writes that, in violence, "young men ritualistically enact an exaggerated version of the gender-role norms expected of men in hypermasculine social environments."[4] Franklin proposes that violence that occurs in these kinds of environments is a form of theater—it is not so much about the victim but rather about the performance of masculinity to other members of the hypermasculine group.

In examining this specific case of Mepham High School—a 2003 hazing incident that included several sexualized elements of anti-gay violence—Franklin writes that the case is a prime example of the theater of masculine power and posturing:

> Older, physically stronger, and more prestigious players engaged in a public display of masculinity, celebrating their strength by violently emasculating their weaker—that is, less manly—teammates. The theatrical element is evident in the requirement of an audience; the laughing approval of this audience provided visible endorsement of the upperclassmen's gendered entitlement. That vilification of the feminine was a core component is

illustrated by the emasculation of the victims, through forcing them to assume the female role in simulated sexual acts as well as through the depilation ritual in which one boy was feminized through the painful removal of his body hair.[5]

The importance of this particular hazing case is that it demonstrates not only the theatrical need for masculinity to be proven through violence, but the ways in which sports culture can be a conduit for such violence and proving of masculinity. Such theater of masculinity is not restricted to the players themselves, but also extends to their fans, as we frequently see behavior among male fans toward women that reflects a brutal and unyielding misogyny. The chain of sexual violence is such that, as Franklin writes, "sexual violence is not an inherent aspect of athletics. Rather sports stars are more likely to commit sexual assaults because of their sense of entitlement and superiority."

When players and their fans are imbued with a specific sense of how masculinity works, sports culture becomes notoriously anti-woman. Important elements of "winning" and "being the best" are exclusive to incorporating any kind of femininity within the sports culture. This is why I get interrogated when I try to sit and watch a game. And this, on a much larger level, is why female sports writers are frequently harassed and threatened simply for doing their jobs, and players who stand up against this culture are reviled.

Let's look at the case of Chris Kluwe, a retired NFL player who spent eight seasons with the Minnesota Vikings and a year with the Oakland Raiders. While he played for the Vikings, his outspokenness on gay rights and marriage equality caused deep tension between him, the coach, and other players. He published several letters in 2012 discussing his support for marriage equality and spoke out openly and actively in favor of LGBT rights. At the end of the 2012 season, he was let go from the Vikings. Two years later, after retiring from football altogether, Kluwe explained in an interview that he was let go because of his vocal support of marriage equality.

He alleged that his coach at the time had used several homophobic slurs in the locker room and specifically called out Kluwe for his support of same-sex marriage.

Kluwe expressed support for marriage equality during a highly contentious time in professional football—marriage quality was not yet the law of the land and of the nearly 1,700 players in professional football, not a single one was out as gay. And, as Kluwe described at the time, a football team was not exactly a group that could discuss such issues with sensitivity. The theater of the masculine was a significant barrier to Kluwe's activism and ultimately, it seems, was a factor in his early retirement from the sport altogether.

Feminist criticism of sports, though it is increasing in both diversity and interest, has classically taken a position of surface-level engagement. We discuss female representation in sports, push for better equality for women in doing the same tasks as men, and for equality of access to programs that offer major benefits to the participants (as student athletes frequently are offered scholarships and their own tutoring centers and the like). It is here, in sports, that we are most likely to be apathetic, lazily labeling it as "problematic" and washing our hands of the matter. What is most lacking is coherent, cohesive connections between toxic masculinity, female rejection of sport, and the fight for equality. We've determined that sports culture is too much, is not worth it, is not going to change—and our criticism therefore reflects it. Jokes about the Super Bowl being a celebration of concussions, mockery of sport as a meaningless venture, and misunderstanding of what events mean to others all seem to exemplify the feminist response to sports culture. But sports are meaningful for many millions of people, and our analysis needs to dive deeper than mere examination of equality within the sport. It's good to support the WNBA. We should also support women involved in male-dominated sports culture.

We are creating and reinforcing the problematic nature of sports in our rejection of the masculine. We not only buy into the worst of sports culture when we do this, but we create a self-fulfilling prophecy where we play into the idea that sports are not places for women. It's a tricky, fine line to walk: to condemn sports culture for their treatment of women while also positioning ourselves as insiders in that culture. It is a line very few can walk, which is why we must support strongly those who can. Sports may not be my thing or your thing. But it is her thing, and she deserves our support, not our scorn for her association with the "problematic."

9

Dinos, Disasters, and Dives

A Feminist Defense of That High-Heeled
Chase Scene in *Jurassic World*

I was introduced to the folk rock band the Decemberists while I was living in Waco, Texas. I remember going to my roommate at the time and telling her that the Decemberists' narratives were modern-day examples of a dramatic monologue in the style of Robert Browning. In Browning's "My Last Duchess," the speaker recounts his relationship to his last wife before revealing himself as her murderer, haunted by her portrait hidden behind curtains on the wall. Likewise, the Decemberists' "Mariner's Revenge Song" uses an old shanty, sailor song style to tell the tale of a sailor, the son of a sex worker, who has spent his life seeking out his father to claim his revenge for leaving his family destitute and disease-ridden. He joins a religious sect, trains to sail, and joins the deserter father on the stormy seas, where they find themselves shipwrecked together—at which point the mariner takes his eponymous revenge. For me, this kind of poetic license was easy to understand, coming from a folk rock band. When I made the connection between Browning and Colin Meloy's lyrics, I excitedly turned to my roommate, a psychology student who had become my friend through our shared interests in theater, literature, and pop culture.

She nodded and agreed, "It's similar with rap music—it's rare anymore that they're actually rapping about crimes and gunfights.

A lot of that was left behind with the murders of Biggie and Tupac."
As a Midwestern white girl, that thought hadn't occurred to me
before—that modern-day popular music was also an area for study,
and that rap music in particular was one of the most imaginative,
most literary genres possible. The idea that I could apply academic
theory and study to such deeply embedded cultural artifacts was a
new one to me at the time, but has since proven itself many times
over as I explore visual theory, popular culture, and feminist critique. Indeed, when I began to identify as a feminist, within a couple of years of this revelation, I was delighted to discover that the
vast majority of feminist understanding was about the application
of theory to culture.

One of the significant barriers to good criticism is accessibility.
The important pieces of art, the important studies, the ability to
simply see and understand what's happening in a popular culture
event—all these tend to be restricted to members of an elite class
who have the education and the understanding to critique it.

Feminist criticism of popular culture is frequently the first and
only encounter many will have with feminism, which places a lot
of power in the hands of the critics. At any point, one critic's feminist take has the possibility of becoming the definitive take on
that piece of art—and thus become a teaching tool for numerous
feminists without access to a comprehensive feminist education.
All too often, however, that "definitive" take morphs into being
the only acceptable vision of the piece of art, rather than just one
more contribution to the conversation that happens to be particularly salient. The translation of physically inaccessible culture into a
mainstream discussion happens because of these critiques. It's part
of the wonder of the internet. Unfortunately, it also means these
critiques have an extraordinarily ability to act as lines in the sand for
feminist discussion. If you don't agree with Jill Filipovic's take on
a certain issue, or if you dare challenge the reading of Lindy West,
you may find yourself on the outs in feminist thought.

Jurassic World is a good example of how this kind of definitive take fanned itself out on a smaller scale. The movie was a new addition to a massive 1990s franchise—one I happen to be a gigantic fan of. My father and I went to see the movie on opening weekend, and we both enjoyed ourselves immensely. The storyline picks up where the first *Jurassic Park* movie left off—the theme park was abandoned, taken over by the animals. A few years after the "accidents," another company came in, cleaned up the island and corralled the dinosaurs again. This company was successful in making John Hammond's "Real Life Dino" theme park come to life.

But, like any theme park, new attractions have to be added every so often to create new interest and new buzz in the park. Claire, a woman with a severe, straight haircut, no maternal instinct, and an incredibly skillful grasp of the ins and outs of her job, has been overseeing the park for a few years and is preparing to reveal a newly created dinosaur to investors. But in a style befitting the franchise creator's original vision, nature finds a way to muck everything up. The new predator dinosaur escapes and wreaks havoc on the park. Claire's nephews go missing and she has to wander out into the jungle—in heels and her business clothes—to try to find and rescue them. In the end, she realizes the only way to survive is to play on nature's food chain—sic one predator on another. She grabs a flare, and runs to the paddock where a *Tyrannosaurus rex* is waiting. In a soon-to-be iconic shot, the door to the paddock slowly moves upward to reveal Claire standing, still in her heels, shaken and bedraggled but with a fierce glint in her eye, holding a lit flare at arm's length, waiting for the roar that signals the *T. rex*'s approach. And soon enough, there it is.

She runs. She runs down an asphalt back road, with a *T. rex* just feet behind her. And she never once takes off her heels.

This iconic moment, this climactic scene—this was the source of deep contention and fury on the part of many feminists. The fact that Claire was running in impractical heels, that she wouldn't bother to take them off, spoke to a seeming inauthenticity with her character—that the concern was much more that she remain beautiful and properly adorned rather than do what any normal woman would, which would be to switch the shoes out for something more practical or just go barefoot. The ensuing controversy was dubbed "Heelgate" by *Cosmopolitan* magazine; and Bryce Dallas Howard, the actress who played Claire, ended up addressing it herself: "She doesn't have to be in menswear and flats to outrun a T-Rex. That's what women can do."[1]

For a time, however, it was very hard to break away from the definitive take on Heelgate, as feminist after feminist argued that the heels represented the beauty restraints placed upon women and Claire's lack of desire to take them off was the result of ongoing pressure to remain perfect even in the face of great danger. Jayson Flores, writing at Bitch Media, wrote an article on "The Five Most Sexist Moments in *Jurassic World*," writing that "because Claire's character is so undeveloped, it feels like her clothes are her only personality. But because her clothes are absurd, given the situation, she seems absurd. In a better-written movie, heels could have been an awesome choice. In this one, they're just silly."[2]

High-heeled shoes have a long and contentious history within feminism, and so it's understandable that feminist critics would balk at the idea of a woman keeping on these symbols of femininity and restrictive beauty ideals and still be proclaimed a hero. It was as though *Jurassic World* triggered some kind of deep level of cognitive dissonance among feminist viewers.

Because the history of symbolic representation and the use of such coding is stolen from academia—ideas about gendered performance, symbolism, and even genderfuck terms like "femme" and "butch" are all based in academic theory—Heelgate becomes hard to sort out. The controversy also follows a pattern of thought and discourse that's all too common in feminist criticism nowadays: someone with just enough knowledge of theory to make some sense inadequately uses that theory to critique a popular artifact.

That interpretation becomes the definitive one, and the theory behind it becomes a game of telephone, where a reading of theory as applied to a specific subject becomes more and more confused as it disseminates. The Bechdel test, invoked during the Heelgate controversy, is one such example of attempted feminist criticism gone awry. It is through the manipulation of such "tests" and the desire to take shortcuts on how we look at criticism that we turn the critique that *is* accessible into *bad critique*. We want people to understand what and how we're critiquing something. But we don't want to do the work to make sure it's translated *correctly*.

In having to both present views to an unsympathetic audience and to avoid going back over basic feminist concepts, many critics end up glossing over the specific ways feminist theory applies to their topics. This results in the skewed understanding of certain theories. This is why "it doesn't pass the Bechdel test" or "she was running in HEEEEELS" has become shorthand for dismissing a movie or TV show, which is a bad misreading of what the both the Bechdel test and symbolic theories actually measure and interpret.

In fact, there have been a number of misguided uses of the Bechdel test in particular, precisely because of the misunderstanding of what the test actually measures and its purpose within feminist criticism. The Bechdel test, invented by writer and artist Alison Bechdel, is a simple test to measure female presence in movies. It does not pass judgment about representation or pronounce whether movies are feminist or not. It simply asks a few questions: Is there more than one *named* female character in the movie? Do those characters have a conversation? Is that conversation about something other than a man? A surprising number of movies fail—and it's that number of failures that's the important measure, not the test of any individual movie. It's not a rating system nor is it a test of feminist credentials. *Jurassic World*, in this instance, passes the test with one conversation: Claire speaks with her sister about their family, including their mother. The argument that it passes the Bechdel test was used as a discussion point for whether or not Heelgate could be read as feminist, further confusing the criticism.

Just a look at the list of a sampling of movies in 2015–16 that do pass the Bechdel test indicates how inappropriate the test is as any kind of rating system for feminism or progressive thinking. *Neighbors 2: Sorority Rising* passes the Bechdel test. *The* DUFF (or Designated Ugly Fat Friend) passes the test. *Fifty Shades of Grey* passes the Bechdel test. All of these feature approval of antifeminist visions of womanhood and not-so-subtle demonizing of women who go outside the feminine mainstream. Meanwhile, Oscar winner *Spotlight* just barely passed the test, with a three-sentence conversation between the one female reporter and her grandmother. But feminism is all over *Spotlight*, as it takes a nuanced and devastating approach to how varied institutions handle cases of child abuse. And, I'd argue, the same is true of *Jurassic World*, where it shows two visions of a woman's life and how different choices can help women to face up to the monsters in our lives.

But the Bechdel test has fallen prey to misinterpretation and misunderstanding on the feminist stage. A movie not passing the test is seen as a mark against it, despite the movie's content. A movie passing it means further exploration of feminist themes may happen. Overall, the test has become an accessible entry point into feminist discussion, but, like many areas of feminist criticism, it has turned into shorthand for actually making a point.

When the test is manipulated to measure the feminism of a piece, as opposed to merely female presence, it can be very easy to assume a black-and-white "this is problematic" attitude about movies based on whether or not they pass this measure. Indeed, many of my favorites don't pass the Bechdel test—the previously discussed *Ex Machina* is a deeply feminist movie that fails the Bechdel test, and it fails the test *on purpose*. A simple data point isn't enough to tell you anything except a sliver of information about that particular data point. But feminist criticism has become very bad at reading data as a whole, and so we learn to, and teach others to, take those data points as individuals, rather than enfolding them into a summation of the whole. We can't look at the whole forest because we're stuck looking at the bark on individual trees.

We develop a cultural understanding of what feminist criticism looks like, and develop ideas of what feminist theory actually is, through these translations of theory into precise acts of criticism. And when these translations, instead of the theories themselves, are taken as gospel, we've set ourselves up for a misunderstood feminism that paints itself into corners because it can't recognize the origin of our specific ideas and place them into context. As I've written previously, divorcing the specific theories from their context has the ability to skew and change that theory into something it's really not.

The *Jurassic World* controversy demonstrates how theory can be divorced from context and taken to be understood in only one particular way. The idea that heels are at once a symbol of empowerment *and* a symbol of oppression is a microcosm of rifts within feminist theory—rifts that take intensive study to work through. I'm speaking mainly of the rift between gender abolitionist feminism and what's been called "choice" or intersectional feminism in a lot of circles. Both of these types of feminists apply their understanding to popular culture, with wildly different results. But because both differing theories are able to position themselves as "feminist" within the mainstream, it takes a very skilled critical eye to differentiate between the two. When we fail to develop feminist skill, when we fail to interact, and instead simply accept, we run the risk of endorsing the problematic in the midst of attempting to destroy it.

Gender abolitionist feminists share a theoretical wheelhouse with trans exclusionary radical feminists (TERFs). The theory disagreement is simple, but has extremely complex rippling effects. Essentially, gender abolitionists believe that the end goal of feminism should be the erasure of gender as a social category altogether. George Gillett, writing in the New Statesman, sums up gender abolitionism thusly:

The existence of gender itself is, by definition, inherently oppressive. The aspects of a gendered identity which one person deems to be positive will equally act to oppress another member of the same sex, who would be unrepresented by such a definition. In fact, the diversity of men and women means that creating a unanimously positive personality type is simply impossible. And even if such an attribute was identified, its association with a specific sex would imply that people of other identities lacked this characteristic. Not only is this concept of gender harmful, but the noxious idea that we can associate a positive set of behavioural characteristics with a physical sex is intrinsically flawed.[3]

The idea, then, is that gender should be abolished entirely. We should see "human" not "female, male, nonbinary, trans, or whatever human." Ironically, many of the women who embrace this philosophy also fall into a strange camp of saying that in order to promote gender abolitionism we need to absolutely and completely forgo the coded feminine. Makeup, nail polish, heels, dresses—all these are symbolic of the oppression of womanhood and we must eschew their effect on our lives in order to become fully realized humans. It is a feminism that says there is an overarching feminist path in life and that deviating from that path makes one antifeminist. Claire continuing to wear her symbols of oppression despite her situation is a symbol of how she is caged by the patriarchy and cannot escape, even when it is life or death.

There's an obvious critique of this idea that comes out of intersectional or choice feminism. This kind of feminism says that every person has intersecting vectors of oppression and privilege—meaning that each person's experience of gender, race, ability, mental health, and sexuality are tied to both their own lived experience and the oppressions and privileges that shape the world in which we all function. I, as a bisexual, cisgender white woman, have a set of oppressions and privileges that interact differently in different ways. The black queer woman marrying her wife in Florida is far different in terms of oppression than what my single white self experiences living in Minnesota. This means that there is no one singularly feminist ideal, but rather a set of oppressions and ways to defeat them hunched up under a big tent of feminism. There are some things that are overwhelmingly feminist or antifeminist, but the individual choices within that moment cannot be read as feminist or antifeminist without the context of that moment. In *Jurassic World*, one has to examine the entire context and journey of Claire's character in order to make a decision about whether or not her running in heels is feminist.

It all depends on your critical lens: what you bring to the piece of popular culture will influence how you read and interpret it. And if you've already been informed that the piece of work is "problematic," that it has been critically received as unfeminist or feminist, it can make it very hard to bring your own reading to the table. Critical application becomes a race to problematize popular culture instead of enacting a slow, critical engagement and thought that adds to the discussion. The cultural artifact that is declared "problematic," based on an individual feminist's reading, is taken as gospel and understood to be the truth. Those ideas sink into the cultural atmosphere, and many avoid what they haven't even seen based on one warning or one reading. This kind of prizing of the first and the fastest and the most condemnatory allows us to short circuit our critical discourse. Problematic becomes our shorthand, and we don't even understand for ourselves that our "problematic" readings are actually rooted in critical theory we'd disagree with if we spent more than two minutes reading about it.

10

Selfie Game Strong

Kim Kardashian and de Beauvoir's
Thoughts on Beauty

I didn't truly understand how much of a global celebrity Kim Kardashian is until I saw her and Kourtney's faces peeking out at me from the side of a London bus. I was there for the weekend and found myself confronted with Kim's face everywhere I went—in the Underground. On the sides of buses. On billboards. When I vacationed in Copenhagen and Berlin later that year, I encountered the same thing—Kim Kardashian's eyes, following me with a slight smile, everywhere I went, even into the bowels of the Danish metro.

Kim Kardashian is the very definition of world famous.

During this same year, my friends and I developed a tradition of hanging out in the common room and having "shitty TV and studying" nights. On a few occasions, the Kardashians would be at the center of that kind of evening, but more often than not, we found ourselves on any one of the strange British TV reality and competition shows—*Big Brother*, *First Dates*, and *Come Dine with Me*. These shows were all documentary style, though one could hardly call them documentaries. In an artificially constructed situation, people interacted with each other in increasingly bizarre (*Take Me Out*) or socially embarrassing ways (*Come Dine with Me*).

Reality television is frequently regarded as the basest of television, the bottom of the barrel. They create artificial situations, ply their protagonists with alcohol, and edit material to create a greater sense of drama than actually exists. Reaction shots from one moment are used for another, and producers stoke stressed-out contestants into full-on rages about misinterpretations and feelings that don't exist, all in the name of ratings.

Reality television is such that Donald J. Trump was able to build on his reality show fame in order to cast himself as a successful, self-made businessman and run for the presidency of the United States. His portrayal of himself on *The Apprentice* as the world's best businessman actually allowed him to retrofit his financial history into a narrative of great business skill. In reality, Trump bankrupted six companies, lost money on a casino (of all things), and generated far less money with his father's "small, million-dollar loan" than he would have had he simply invested it. But the "reality" of reality television is that it allows for this reimagining of the self.

For years, *The Apprentice* was just a harmless show. People watched or didn't watch, and no one paid any real attention to how Trump was using the show to reinvent his image and himself. That is, until 2016, when many realized, far too late, that he really did see himself as a successful businessman. It was too late to get those "alternative facts" changed. We had spent so long dismissing him that taking him seriously now seemed like a wild proposition. This is not to say that we need to pay attention to *Jersey Shore* because The Situation might decide to run for office, but that blanket dismissal of reality television can cause us to lose connection with a large part of the American psyche.

By dismissing them, we also end up handing reality TV stars their greatest freedoms. Because doing things outside the norm is par for the course on reality television, the ability to create in fascinating ways is an uncharted path. We can both toe the line of traditional gendered roles while also flouting them in the very setup of the show, and we can center women of color who have turned a source of shame into a source of revenue in a giant middle finger to the industry.

And there's plenty to critique in reality TV. One trope that's particularly common and highly visible in reality television is the parsing out of standards for feminine beauty. Contestants on *The Bachelor* vary pretty much only in hair color. Contestants on the physically and mentally taxing show *The Amazing Race* are mostly fit models from LA. The Real Housewives of Whatever City in Randomly Picked State all seem to fit particular molds of having typically feminine characteristics.

The most pernicious of shows that is entirely based on this upholding of thin and beautiful is *The Biggest Loser*. NBC's megahit reality show features contestants who are, according to the narrative of the show, obscenely overweight and compete to see who can lose the most weight (in proportion to their starting weight). The transformations at the end of the show are, in fact, stunning, but also serve to give us an inaccurate and badly skewed view of what weight loss actually looks like. Contestants on the show sign binding nondisclosure agreements, but many have flouted those contracts in favor of spreading the truth about what happens on the show.

Contestants are forced to work out all day, every day, and kept on nearly starvation diets. They are asked to exercise well beyond a body's natural stopping point in an effort to fit within the time constraints of the show. The new diets they are put on are not nearly enough calories to keep a person's body going when they are exercising that much, so the body is essentially forced into shock for the duration of the show. Many contestants have exited the show with deeply damaging eating disorders, unable to allow themselves to eat the amount of calories a body needs to be healthy.

As often happens after a major weight loss like those featured during the show, the body begins to yo-yo between weights, meaning a contestant will almost assuredly and immediately begin gaining back the weight lost. And yet, this "reality" show is immensely popular, with high ratings—because it sells us this idea that transforming our bodies can make us happy. Fitting into ideal beauty standards that somehow correspond to "health" is immensely popular because of how it promises us fame and fortune and happiness for doing so.

It's a toxic message, but it's all too common in reality shows. The most beautiful girl on *The Bachelor* gets to marry the rich guy. The person who has the greatest transformation wins millions on *The Biggest Loser*. It's inspiration pornography—we look at surrogates for our own desire for transformation and see what we could be ourselves.

This is why, I argue, the Kardashians are such an important family for what they are doing with reality television, and media criticism is wrong to use them as a frequent punch line.

The Kardashian family has always been fame-adjacent. In the early 1990s, the patriarch of the family, Robert, was part of O.J. Simpson's legal team and rocketed into national recognition because of his role in the trial. By that time, he'd already divorced his first wife, Kris, and left her with custody of their four children: Kim, Khloe, Kourtney, and Rob. When the O.J. trial rolled around, Kris had remarried the famous Olympian, Bruce Jenner, who came out in 2014 as a transgender woman named Caitlyn Jenner.

But it was Kim, the second daughter of Kris and Robert, who really brought the family to fame—in a uniquely scandalous and, for feminists, fascinating way. While Kim was dating R&B singer Ray J, they recorded a private sex tape. That tape leaked four years later (long after they'd broken up). As reports flew about the rumored sex tape, Kim did a remarkable thing: she didn't run and hide, but instead told *Hollywood Extra* at the time: "A tape does exist . . . whatever we did was our personal business, and I hope that it remains private." When the family began filming their reality show later that same year, she parlayed the controversy over her sex tape into attention on the show, slyly making her name as a reality show star.

A decade after the release of the sex tape, Kim is one of the most recognized stars in the world. She is married to rapper Kanye West and has two kids with him. She has turned her successes in reality TV to success in business—she has a ton of endorsement deals, her own lines of clothing and perfumes and jewelry, and has marketed herself as a brand so well that people instantly recognize it. She is a force to be reckoned with.

And it all started with a sex tape, the kind of scandal that had brought down many women before her.

In his book *So You've Been Publicly Shamed*, Jon Ronson proposes that the reason some people seem untouched by shaming spectacles is that they have simply stopped caring. In an exchange with Max Mosley, a British celebrity who was the victim of an attempted public shaming about a consensual kinky sex party he had, Ronson asked him how he got away with it. Mosley's response was simple: "As soon as the victim steps out of the pact by refusing to feel ashamed, the whole thing crumbles."[1]

This is quite similar to what Kim Kardashian did—she confirmed the existence of the sex tape, said her part, and then went on with her life. She refused to be defined by what many prudish people would call dirty and what the rest of the public would call salacious. This lack of ability to be shamed has served Kim Kardashian well over the years, as she simply shrugged off things people said about her and broadcast her life on national television, practically inviting criticism.

Kardashian's "water off a duck's back" approach to criticism is one worth learning from—criticism from the public, especially a public crowing for public shaming because someone has failed to be perfect, isn't necessarily worth listening to. Throughout the show, it's clear that she has people in her life that she prioritizes and whose critiques she will listen to—often resulting in some dramatic television when they butt heads. But what Kim demonstrates is actually a fairly healthy attitude toward criticism and fame.

One of the criticisms Kim faces down daily is that she prizes her own beauty and her own body too much. She takes too many selfies! She's obsessed with contouring and makeup tips. She, supposedly, is leading women to see their worth in their beauty. A feminist culture focused on "protecting women" has leveled this criticism at

Kim multiple times, ironically mirroring a mainstream patriarchal culture. This cultural synchronicity between criticisms should be a warning sign for feminists: if you find yourself agreeing with Piers Morgan, you should probably reexamine your priorities.

In late 2013, after the famed *Oxford English Dictionary* declared "selfie" as their "word of the year," feminist journalist Erin Gloria Ryan wrote an article for a feminist celebrity magazine decrying selfies as "a cry for help," not empowerment. She declared, emphatically, "Stop this. Selfies aren't empowering; they're a high tech reflection of the fucked up way society teaches women that their most important quality is their physical attractiveness." Ryan then developed a taxonomy of selfies, in which she eliminates selfies designed to show off a product of some kind as "not pure selfies."[2] Ryan's taxonomy allows her to dictate what is and is not appropriate. The point of a selfie, to Ryan, is to show one's face to the world for no other reason than that it exists. And, as Ryan expounds, it serves as a cry for help from others, because posting a selfie apparently means you're lonely.

Ryan goes after teenage girls and their obsession with the selfie viciously:

> Young women take selfies because they don't derive their sense of worth from themselves, they rely on others to bestow their self-worth on them—just as they've been taught. From the time they're itty bitty, little girls are bombarded with the images of idealized female forms. They're indoctrinated with Victoria's Secret–style cartoonishly unobtainable passive Sexiness and told that this is what they should Be When They Grow Up. They're being sold "flirty" child-sized Halloween costumes modeled after "sexy" adult costumes. They're told that they're at their best when they're at their most decorative.

I grew up not liking my face. I have a pronounced, hooked nose that my family jokingly calls "the Anderson nose." It took me years to grow into it, and a few more years to be comfortable with seeing my own face in the mirror. Now, I happily take selfies while working, while out on the town, while just sitting with my cat. I'm happy to post pictures of myself doing the most mundane of things, and I no longer cringe when I see my own face. I no longer want to pick apart my own image.

Ryan, here, is setting up the selfie, as a cry to be seen, as entirely an object. Her ideas rest, unconsciously, on feminist subject theory. We are that which the male subject determines—we are the object of the male's gaze. According to Ryan, creating media that buys into that objectification is playing into the subjugation of the self, even as we make the self more prominent. In one of the most important works of Western feminism, the French philosopher Simone de Beauvoir writes:

> Meting out blame and approbation is useless. In fact, the vicious circle is so difficult to break here because each sex is a victim both of the other and of itself; between two adversaries confronting each other in their pure freedom, an agreement could easily be found, especially as this war does not benefit anyone; but the complexity of this whole business comes from the fact that each camp is its enemy's accomplice; the woman pursues a dream of resignation, the other for unhappiness brought upon himself by taking the easy way out; what the man and the woman hate in each other is the striking failure of their own bad faith and cowardice.[3]

One of the lessons of de Beauvoir's *Second Sex* is that women are complicit in their own oppression at times because man has made it seem desirable to give up our femininity—to divorce ourselves from the signals of our sex, the feminine, the "silly, girly things." We have learned to look at ourselves through a lens of how it may please others and not how we ourselves might be pleased.

One of the great benefits of these somewhat narcissistic times is that it's created a healthy dose of narcissism among people who have been taught to do everything in their lives for others. When we look at ourselves more and become confident in putting our images out in the world, not only do we inspire confidence in others, but we inspire confidence in ourselves.

This is at least part of why I count Kim Kardashian among those who *should* be role models for children, because, although some would call her career self-obsessed narcissism, she has demonstrated a healthy love of self, a resistance to being shamed, and ownership of herself and her business. Like Beyoncé, who carefully controls her public image, Kim's flaunting of herself before the public eye creates a relationship in which she asks that people gaze, but she also controls that gaze.

Indeed, when Kim published an entire coffee table book, titled *Selfie*, that was almost exclusively compiled of pictures of herself, she made a statement that was at once asking people to look at her and controlling how they looked. She leaned into the conceptions of herself as an attention-seeking woman and happily gave it the middle finger by ensuring that we had enough to look at and judge. De Beauvoir, decades prior to the advent of the Kardashians, actually commented on the particular phenomenon of the woman as actress, or, nowadays, as reality star:

There is one category of woman to whom these remarks do not apply because their careers, far from harming the affirmation of their femininity, reinforce it; through artistic expression they seek to go beyond the very given they constitute; actresses, dancers, and singers. For three centuries they have almost been the only ones to possess concrete independence in society, and today they still hold a privileged place in it. In the past, actresses were cursed by the Church: this excessive severity allowed them great freedom of behavior; they are often involved in seduction, and like courtesans they spend much of their days in the company of men: but as they earn their living themselves, finding meaning in the existence of their work, they escape men's yoke. Their great advantage is that their professional success contribute—as for males—to their sexual worth; by realizing themselves as human beings, they accomplish themselves as women: they are not torn between contrary aspirations.[4]

Kardashian's work blends directly into the current debate over the performance of femininity within feminism. There are multiple factions under the large umbrella of feminist thought, but one of the largest current divides is between intersectional choice feminism and gender critical or gender abolitionist feminism, as discussed in the previous chapter.

Feminine-performing women, or femmes, don't find space within gender abolitionism because they are immediately written off as shallow, as performing for men, as developing their sense of self-worth in an externalized, outmoded sense of their own gender. When engaging in critique of Kim Kardashian as performing for the male gaze, typically intersectional feminists are engaging in a gender abolitionist argument. Trans women, in particular, are attacked by this kind of feminism for passing—or for performing femininity in an effort to be what trans exclusionary radical feminists call "real women."

It should be noted that according to the vast majority of gender theory and thought, transgender women are women and transgender men are men because gender is at once socially constructed and an innate sense of self. Gender, developed socially and understood by cues that are situationally oppressive (more on this in a second), is also an innate sense of who we are as human beings. Gender is therefore malleable and changeable and dependent upon both individual feelings and social cues.

Gender abolitionist and trans exclusionary feminism dictates that these performances of femininity must be left behind if we hope to achieve a postgender feminism in which we women are truly equal with men. The argument, unfortunately, has a hole large enough to drive a Mack truck through: in order to argue that we must give up on feminine expressions and ideals of gender to develop postgender lives, these radical feminists are essentially arguing that we should become men: Develop male social cues and leanings, express our gender in ways that are coded male, and despise the femininity of other women. Entrench the patriarchy further by despising femininity and eventually we will rid the world of gender altogether.

This, obviously, will not do, but this is the section of feminism that seeks to punish Kim Kardashian for being a deeply feminine and image-driven woman. Her choices as a smart businesswoman who knows how to capitalize on her—ahem—assets become relegated to the perpetuation of an antifeminist misogyny because the performance of femininity must only exist to please men.

But this kind of feminism, naturally, depends on the elevation of the group over the individual—something feminism, especially intersectional feminism, is desperately trying to avoid. Antifemininity, when encoded into conceptions of feminism, is deeply antiwoman. This is not to say that performances of femininity are inherently female but that they are situationally coded as such and can therefore be turned about to be used as weapons in the rebellion against gender. Kim Kardashian, as a woman of color (she is Armenian) who has made a business of performing availability and femininity, has perfected that rebellion by performing it so well.

For many women, especially women who don't naturally fit into beauty standards or whose beauty is viewed as existing for a consumptive white male gaze, the femininity performed by someone like Kim Kardashian can actually be refreshing. When she posts a naked selfie from her hotel room and gets shamed about it by Piers Morgan on social media, she is challenging images of what it means to be a woman in modern society. We're still required to be prim, proper, and innocent. Kim challenges that at every turn.

The very thing that helped her become a household name—not her sex tape, but her reality show—is an important demonstration of how popular culture can aid in the humanizing of women. On her reality show, she allows herself to be shown in ridiculous situations, saying things that are kind of begging to be mocked, and yet she brazenly doesn't care. She's a human woman who controls her image, and part of that image is showing herself as a silly, ridiculous human.

In one particularly memorable moment, Kim and her new husband travel with the family to Bora Bora. Her husband grabs her and throws her into the ocean off the dock, causing her very expensive earrings to fall out—earrings worth nearly one hundred thousand dollars. And she, like any person who just lost a massively expensive object would do, starts crying.

And the worldwide response to her is deeply misogynistic. She's "freaking out," as her husband says in the show. News reports about it show the clip in order to mock her. People blamed her by asking "Who wears expensive jewelry to the beach?" and her own family mocked her in the moment.

Kim takes a lot of hits, in other words. A perfectly natural reaction to something bad happening is blasted around the world and opened up for mockery. But Kim's willingness to air her life out like this demonstrates to the world that someone performing femininity excellently is also a capable human being with feelings and thoughts and ideas. This refusal to be reduced to a caricature is a feminist choice, and Kardashian is demonstrating more of that rebellion than people recognize.

Kardashian's femme rebellion, in my mind, sits alongside the performances of such stars as Rita Hayworth, a notably fiery young woman who used femininity to her advantage both on and off the screen. In her most famous film, *Gilda*, she plays a femme fatale in a casino in Argentina. The first time anyone in the film sees her, it's from the back—a mysterious woman in the middle of a group of men, walking confidently across the casino floor. The famous film noir piece, which has entered into the U.S. National Film Registry as a movie of "significant cultural and aesthetic value," banks on Gilda's femininity as the crux of the movie. Both the male protagonists love and abuse her in their own ways, manipulating and using her beauty for their own gains. But in the same moment, she uses her beauty to get the upper hand—when her husband fakes his death, she inherits everything and gains control. When her next husband tries to keep her on a short leash, she becomes creative and uses her femininity to taunt him in front of other men.

In one of the most famous sequences in the film, Gilda puts on a sexy black dress and sidles out onto the casino floor. She calls up the band and begins to sing—and then begins to perform a strip tease, all the while singing an old standard, "Put the Blame on Mame." The song asks that the audience blame several natural disasters and famous accidents on a fictional woman named "Mame," whose womanly wiles were so powerful that she caused the Frisco quake.

At the end of her tune, Gilda keeps the audience's gaze by slowly removing one of her long gloves and ripping off her choker necklace. In a half-joking but also serious declaration, she takes a bow and declares, "I'm not very good at zippers, but maybe if I had some help!"[5] Several men in the audience leap forward, but before they can, her husband's men step in and take her out. On the way, she tries to kiss one of the men who offered to help her with her zipper. The laughing crowd is silent when her husband appears. And they fight:

JOHNNY: What do you mean by it?
GILDA: Now they all know what I am. And that should make you happy, Johnny! It's no use just you knowing it, Johnny! Now they all know that the mighty Johnny Farrell got taken! And he married a wh—

[Johnny slaps her, cutting her off][6]

The unspoken word there is, obviously, "whore." She knows exactly how she's perceived, she knows how to weaponize her femininity to shame her husband for his behavior toward her, and she does it in ways that discombobulate and decimate the narrative of women as decorations. Women have, for ages, used their femininity and the underestimations that come alongside it in order to undermine and fight back against patriarchal cages.

This is largely, I maintain, what Kim Kardashian is doing by maintaining a deeply feminine image and airing her dirty laundry on TV. Just as Gilda holds up a mirror to Johnny's brutality, so Kim Kardashian holds up a mirror to our deepest impulses of hatred toward women—particularly women of color. Whether or not she does this purposefully is a question for debate, but I choose to believe she's a lot smarter than people give her credit for. Her narcissistic femininity creates a foil to the patriarchal conceptions of the selfless and effortlessly beautiful woman. The discounting of her work as important to feminist culture costs us a potential ally—simply because her image is problematic.

Kardashian's weaponized femininity is actually a largely feminist statement, and one we discount at our peril. She is facilitating the humanization of femmes everywhere, handing us methods of expression and ways to understand ourselves. And thanks to her reality show, she's also showing us that it's not a bad idea to cry sometimes, even full-on ugly crying. Because we're human women, and emotions are part of our discourse and our lives, and yes, our femininity.

11

Pinterest Perfect

How Our Home Lives Reflect an
Unhealthy Obsession

During my time working at a daycare, I had lots of conversations with moms who clearly felt pressure to be the perfect mom. Everything from the birthday treats children brought in to their outfits were attempts at being that picture-perfect family. One mom was so obsessed with her daughter's fashion that she would not allow the kid to go into the sandbox because she risked getting her beautiful, fashionable clothes dirty.

Her kid was two.

Another mom opened up to me about where she got all her ideas: "It's an idea I got from Pinterest," she'd say as she handed me a box of carefully decorated cookies for her daughter's birthday. "This one kind of failed, but they still taste good." I looked in the box and saw what must have been her "fail"—some of the swirls in the cookies had extended out so the concentric circles were more like rings in a tree and not a carefully woven rug. And that was it.

The cookies were delicious, regardless.

I don't have children (and don't plan to), but I've been mom-adjacent for a while, thanks to my two nieces and multiple baby second cousins. And one of the things that comes up when discussing kids with my friends who are new to motherhood is the pressure to be "Pinterest Perfect." If you can't take a good, well-lit picture and share it on social media, how good of a mom are you?

This pressure is, always and forever, aimed at mothers. Fathers are still, by and large, characterized as babysitters when they parent. Despite increasing gender equality that means more women are working outside the home, there is increased social pressure to perform both tasks perfectly in the pursuit of not only having great children, but making sure you can brag about them online.

In this vein, the past few years have seen a huge proliferation of television shows and programs focused on the domestic sphere. Both HGTV and Food Network have become immensely popular cultural mainstays, with top shows on each network becoming household names. Their preeminence was bound to happen—even when I was a child, decorating and food-focused shows were immensely popular. American influence has extended overseas, where the UK imports DIY Network, and its most-watched television show is *The Great British Bake Off*, a food-focused competition among amateur bakers.

But the devotion to presenting the domestic sphere in both competitive and picture-perfect ways is unique to the American television obsession. Even on *Great British Bake Off*, the competition is focused much more on taste and texture than on presentation. One of the largest controversies on one season of the show centered around one contestant throwing out his dish after his presentation didn't turn out the way he wanted it to. "Ian, we could have still tasted it and judged your baking on that!" the judges told him as they eliminated him from competition.[1] It didn't matter, not fully, what the food looked like, as long as the taste was still there. In America, the contestant's move would have been seen as somewhat normal.

It's not just an outsider perception that America is obsessed with food. Our portion sizes are measurably larger than those found in Europe, and we have more television shows devoted to food preparation than any other country. We consume an immense amount of food and contribute even more to food waste.[2]

America's strange relationship with food manifests itself in innumerable ways and has distinct, unique methods of delineating between rich and poor, black and white, and fat and skinny. As we joke about eating disorders that models have, we also judge fat people if they're on a diet, refusing to diet, or cheating on a diet. We use food to judge the actions of the poor, even restricting what food stamps can and cannot be used for. And we watch both good and bad chefs on television, equally obsessed with both.

Television is a literal companion in many people's homes. It's on there in the background as we do our work, it's entertainment in the evenings, it's a constant presence in our lives. Food television becomes important for many of us because it forms an aspirational bond with us: we see what we are not but hope to become. Many of the shows promise an image of domestic life that does not reflect our own lives, let alone our own dining room tables. There is a political exchange of power that happens through our obsession with food: we express class, race, and ableist power based on our food intake and our food presentation. For my family, having steamed crab in the shell is a treat reserved for special occasions (and only then when the crab is on sale). We've never made lobster at home. But for others, it's a normal fact of life. Television that is focused on the domestic sphere, whether it's Food Network or HGTV, sets standards of what a certain class of people should hope to be or experience.

Many of us in white America don't recognize this exchange of power because power within the domestic-focused industry is so diffuse and invisible. Our obsession with food television aids in this diffusion of power because we normalize and welcome the focus on waste of food. A judge on a food show takes one or two bites before shoving an entire plate of food away. A dish cooked for demonstration typically sees the inside of a trashcan instead of someone's belly. Despite evidence that one in five children in

America is food-insecure—meaning they don't have an assured access to food throughout the day—America continues to obsess over food *and* insist on its apolitical nature.[3] Food culture becomes part and parcel of cultural expression—and is seen as somehow less important than things "actually affecting" people's lives. It is an invisible force, only brought to the surface in salient moments, like when the president of the United States uses a moment discussing the bombing of Syria to rave about the piece of chocolate cake he was eating when it happened.[4]

HGTV, likewise, highlights the most extravagant portions of wasteful lifestyle living: getting a summer home in Belize, buying and "flipping" a house for profit, redoing basements into extravagant and unnecessary "man caves." The trend toward aspirational beauty has deeply impacted how we Americans view ourselves, our homes, and our food.

These discussions are entirely political, as well. No aspirational pressure exists outside of a classist form of political hierarchy: those with the money to pay for fancy kitchens and expensive ingredients are the most prized. And this extends to discussions of who can or cannot eat the food. In one particular episode of *Chopped*, the contestants are all amateur "lunch lady" cooks. The judges are all people who have experience with childhood nutrition through various charities and programs they participate in. One cook knows her school's student body really well and talks about how, at her school, Mondays are always heavy pasta days because pasta is filling and helps satiate hunger—and she knows this because she has several students who don't get a solid meal over the weekend, so they're hungry when they come in on Monday.[5]

In one of the challenges, she makes a massive bowl of pasta and dishes out generous portions to the judges. One of the judges remarks that the portion sizes are outside what would typically be healthy for a child because childhood obesity is an epidemic.

This focus on preventing obesity over and above preventing hunger demonstrates, importantly, our strange and warped relationship to food: it is more important to many people in positions of power that we *not* have fat kids than that we *have* hungry kids. If there's one thing American media doesn't like, even as we obsess over it, is people eating "too much." America really hates fat people.

An entire field of studies—referred to as "corpulence studies"—has sprung up to counter ideas of fatness as a moral evil and to engage with cultural artifacts that simultaneously encourage and discourage an obsession with food. Josee Johnston and Judith Taylor summed it up thusly: "Corpulence studies identifies agency, everyday forms of resistance, and the varied ways gender is constructed in bodies that defy idealized feminine beauty."[6] How we relate to food in the everyday popular culture fits under this area of study, informing how we construct our images of agentic humans and what fat people experience. This area of study is particularly relevant for women who watch thin, beautiful women cook amazing food with thousands of calories and never gain any weight. The aspiration is not only to be a good cook who produces beautiful food, but to be a skinny cook who remains a perfect image of feminine beauty.

In a case study examining how bodies are portrayed in the media, Taylor and Johnston dissect a series of commercials produced by Dove, beginning in 2004. As part of a mainstreaming of feminist ideals, Dove started a "campaign for real beauty," in which they showed women of different sizes dancing around and being generally happy in their skins. The commercialized product, as Taylor and Johnston explain, is part of the mainstreaming of feminist cultural values, a push against the narrow beauty ideals imposed upon women.

But, Johnston and Taylor point out, the campaign still lands on a demand that women value beauty as an important attribute of their lives. "Women's acceptance of their bodies as beautiful is demanded," the authors write, "rather than recognized as an inherently complex, fraught and contradictory endeavor."[7] Even within supposedly positive messages about our bodies, we still are charged with accepting the idea that our beauty is what matters. With our obsessions with food and weight loss and control of appetites, it's no surprise that beauty and looks still factor into the equation. This is why it's so devastating that many feminists ignore food television or regard it as benign. The importance of critiquing not just the food world but the entire "lifestyle" television genre is of vital importance to anyone wishing to translate and discuss feminist issues on the world stage. One cannot address the political and human issues without being willing to address the innumerable ways in which women are instructed to exist.

We, as feminists, are not immune to this kind of discussion. We've been getting better about being inclusive of fat activism, but our celebration and criticism of this area of television is still lacking, largely because we struggle with developing a feminist voice on the topic. We reserve this kind of television for mockery, refusing to delve all that much deeper into what it's actually saying about American consumerist culture and societal pressures to have that picture-perfect Thanksgiving dinner or Christmas decoration. What is the feminist take on Food Network and HGTV? Is it simply connecting it back to body image? Is it this angle of aspiration? Or are we missing something larger? Have we simply written it off as problematic and therefore mockable?

One of the insidious ways we fail in terms of feminist criticism is the ongoing mockery of HGTV's *House Hunters* and *House Hunters International*. The show's premise is simple: in an entirely fabricated set up, a couple looks for a new home that is blocks from the beach and yet still close to work (or some other absurd ideal). Comedian John Mulaney actually delivered a great example of the ways in which popular critics tend to approach these kinds of shows: "Every episode of HGTV is like: Craig and Stasia are looking for a two-story A frame that's near Craig's job in the downtown but also satisfies Stasia's desire to be near the beach, which is nowhere near Craig's job. With three children and nine on the way, and a max budget of seven dollars, let's see what Lori Jo can do on this week's episode of 'You Don't Deserve a Beach House.'"[8]

Mulaney's exaggerated hilarity encapsulates the tone of the criticism aimed at HGTV and those shows whose primary audience is women. The shows encourage us to develop this idea of who deserves something and who doesn't and use it to critique and mock programs that highlight people we consider undeserving. There's a distinct tinge of class resentment and response to the aspirational ideal that colors how we approach (and mock) shows like *House Hunters*: we dislike that those who are better off than many of us can just up and move to Iceland or South Korea or any market with rents and housing costs too high for 99 percent of the world. The undercurrent is that these people have some kind of flaw that makes it so they are no longer deserving of that thing they've worked hard for. This is especially the case with *Tiny House Hunters*, as that show—wherein people are looking for a mobile home the size of my bedroom—is criticized for gentrifying the mobile home, which is typically coded as a "white trash" kind of environment. HGTV engages and invokes concerns over gentrification, class struggle, race, and gender relations, all without necessarily intending to.

Journalist Doree Shafrir wrote an extensive piece about the Tiny House trend on BuzzFeed, pointing out that Tiny House owners usually pay cash or manage to finance a loan (not necessarily a traditional mortgage) for their new homes. These options aren't available to a lot of people, while the Tiny House community—there is a community, as with anything—promotes their style of living as green, easy, and accessible. Shafrir writes:

> "Going tiny" implies that the person who is moving into a tiny house is doing so to escape their previous life of excess: They are coming from one place and going to another. This has made it, by definition, a middle-class movement, one that eschews identification with people who have lived in "tiny" homes for

decades—whether that "tiny" home is a mobile home, an RV, or just a really small apartment. And so the tiny house movement has an inherent privilege built in: Going tiny is a *choice*. If you're coming from a more abundant place, in which you *could* live in a 2,000-square-foot house but you *choose* to live in 200 square feet, then you can be part of the community. If not, well, you're just poor.[9]

The ways in which HGTV and other networks capitalize on the Tiny House movement have elicited mockery from numerous feminist critics—mockery that rarely moves from jokes into actual, searing criticism of these new cultural artifacts we find in both the Tiny House movement and the televised interest in the peculiarly American action of owning one's own home instead of renting from someone else. Such mockery seems to assume an audience already aware of the criticism and therefore not in need of understanding and elucidating it further.

But this would be a mistake. In assuming that we all share the same critical stance, we make a dangerous assumption about our community that stalls critical thinking and delving deeper into important issues that face us every day. The Tiny House movement and *House Hunters International* are good inroads to the discussion of gentrification, especially with a white middle-class audience. But if we're not engaging our fellow audience members in that discussion, we're doing so at a significant opportunity cost. We're letting our jokes and our shrugging off the shows as "problematic" do all the work of critical thinking for us.

We see this same failure of discussion and critical thinking in our approaches to various food-based television shows. One of the Food Network shows that I absolutely love to watch is Alton Brown's *Cutthroat Kitchen*. On the show, four chefs are given $25,000 each to spend on various "sabotages" throughout the competition. All the chefs have to prepare the same dish, and they have the opportunity to buy methods of manipulating the competition—the sabotages. These sabotages range from the small but evil—not allowed to taste your dish—to the downright diabolical—having to prepare your dish while sitting upright in a coffin. A judge eliminates one contestant at the end of each round (without any knowledge of the sabotages) and the last contestant gets to keep whatever money they have remaining from that initial $25,000.

The show, however, has frequently and somewhat accidentally developed a fascinating gender dynamic. The contestants are encouraged to talk smack about each other and to each other throughout the show, and it typically remains in the friendly sphere—the "hey batta batta" of chef speak. But at least a few times a season, when male and female chefs go head-to-head, there will frequently be a male chef who seems to take a special liking to harassing the (often sole) female chef. Commentary about motherhood, about how "weak" a certain chef is, and sometimes physical intimidation will color the show, giving it a distinctly terrible flavor. The show demonstrates an unintended consequence of unchecked sexism: the rates at which female contestants win versus male contestants is nearly a one to two ratio.[10]

But because shows aimed at the domestic scene—even shows helmed by men and frequently won by men—are considered items for mockery and not for serious thought, criticism has failed to develop a solid rubric for understanding these "fun" shows. This is doubled by the fact that these shows give us a safe way to mock women for doing domestic things traditionally seen as women's work. Food Network chef Mario Batali is a large, ginger man who became famous (and mocked in his own way) for his Food Network shows that featured him wearing Croc shoes in the kitchen. In the introduction to fellow Food Network chef Giada De Laurentiis's cookbook, Batali exemplifies the gross sexualization that women who appear even in domestic-focused shows have to put up with: "The first thing I noticed was that everything on the screen was beautiful—both the host and the food, which looked delicious and real and natural. Then I noticed that she really knew what she was talking about. And I realized that despite her movie-star looks, Giada isn't on television because she's merely attractive; she's a real Italian girl who can cook."[11] Andrea Grimes, a food blogger at Resistance Kitchen and former journalist at the *Texas Observer*, brought this to my attention, with the commentary that De Laurentiis is, in placing this at the front of her cookbook in the preface, demonstrating what women have to undergo to make it in these Hollywood-ized food shows.[12]

All this gets worse with the treatment of women who are not under a size ten. Fat chefs are fine if they're men, but fatter women seem to struggle more on the shows and are held up for mockery more frequently. For example, it's fairly common on episodes of *Cutthroat Kitchen* for a fat female chef to be sabotaged with some kind of ridiculous costume that forces her to be more physical than she normally would in her work. It's not uncommon to watch a female chef sweat and turn bright red as she tries to work around the kitchen in a suit of armor or a sumo wrestling fat suit. The extended joke of the moment is "Ha ha, look at this fat person sweating."

And we gobble it up as audience members. I keep returning to the show like a horse to a stream. I watch it consistently, frequently while I'm doing my own cooking, because the jokes are funny, and it's fun to see people overcome immense obstacles and challenges. For the most part, the show is solid, offering wholesome, unique challenges to skilled chefs who have forgotten more knowledge of the kitchen than I could dream of having. But watching such television does require disengaging from my critical mind. I find myself saying the show is "problematic" and refusing to do any more work to explore why. I shorthand myself in my desire to allow myself to like The Thing.

Food competition shows are less outright aspirational than the HGTV house hunting and redecoration programs, but they still function on the basic premise of prizing the middle class, prizing things that are inaccessible to most, and preserving the whiteness of both the kitchen and the home. These shows, objects of our mockery and scorn and fascination, are all too often relics of the wider attitudes toward the domestic sphere. We feminists have missed a larger opportunity by focusing our criticism not on the promotion of gentrification, not on corpulence studies, not on the mockery and objectification of female chefs, but on the sheer mockable gendered aspects. The most common sentiment I see from my fellow feminists about shows like HGTV's *House Hunters* is a joke about the couple divorcing before the end of the show. This deeply gendered aspect of our mockery undermines the work that feminists are encouraged to do in order to think critically and thoughtfully about the world around us. We seem to reserve our mockery for the sphere many of us have escaped—our deepest scorn is for other women still involved in the domestic sphere and this leaches into what we value as entertainment and as necessary areas for criticism. Our hatred of the domestic extends to our biting mockery of gender politics on HGTV and our love of jokey but sexist shows like *Cutthroat Kitchen*. Feminists seem to lack an ability to move from sheer mockery to thoughtful criticism of television shows based upon the domestic sphere. Critique—even heavy-handed, "problematic" critique—is reserved almost exclusively for the male-helmed prestige projects. A love and affection for anything else, especially if it's helmed by a feminine figure, is an object for mockery, first, and critique, second, if at all.

This hierarchy extends beyond HGTV and Food Network, but is most exemplified by our approach to them. On an intellectual level, many feminists seem to recognize the need for food to be politicized and understood as a political element of cultural expression. But when it comes to the necessity of such critique, feminists seem to lean much more heavily upon mockery than on serious, thoughtful evaluation. Indeed, while there seems to be genuine appreciation for Food Network and HGTV among feminists, simple searches of research databases yield little to no actual critical analysis of the shows. We're simply not moving the criticism beyond the Twitter-sphere mockery, where popular insults get thousands of retweets. We are letting "problematic" do all the heavy lifting for us.

This is, in many ways, a subconscious expression of the feminist rejection of the domestic sphere. We don't like the idea that these shows may be designed to appeal particularly to women—and that a lot of women do watch them. We perhaps realize that many of these shows, especially the food shows, are tilted in favor of men. And we don't think critically about where that discomfort is coming from, so we turn to mockery. This is not to say that mockery never has its place, but that in our criticism of the domestic sphere, mockery has become a replacement for critical thought, which is a failure of critique.

When we mock, we have to ask ourselves why we are defaulting to it, why we see it as a reasonable response. Is there something more we can be doing here? Or does mockery achieve the effect we were looking for? If not, why not? This is critical thinking. This is asking ourselves for deeper thought, for understanding, both of ourselves and the object we're critiquing.

12

"I Am Big Enough to Admit I Am Often Inspired by Myself"

Leslie Knope as the Paragon of Feminist Joy

In the summer of 2016, I took a job as a field organizer for the Iowa Democratic Party. I was recruiting and organizing volunteers in rural Iowa, driving back and forth between coffee shops, living off the junkiest fast food and gas station coffee and free Wi-Fi wherever I could find it. I knocked on doors until my hands bled and developed headache after headache making phone calls until the sun went down. About halfway through this short contract job, my boss asked me if everything was okay, because I hadn't been smiling as much on our morning Google Hangouts.

An active career in politics has the ability to sap all the happy right out of a person—there's some crisis to solve every morning when you wake up, and every volunteer has their own ideas about how things should be done—very few of which are actually good ideas. There comes a moment when you text your boss that HQ needs a budget for bail money soon because if one more person asks you why you don't have yard signs available, you may just start swinging.

One of the things that kept me going during this time was a set of coworkers who were brilliant, good at their jobs, encouraging, and, most importantly, made me laugh. Whenever we had chances to get together, our conversations were filled with the laughter of inside jokes, knowing eye rolls about the attitudes of certain volunteers, and stories about the state of the campaign. We turned our complaints into a source of laughter, our frustrations into a thing we could absolve with a good giggle and a high five. We never lost sight of the importance of what we were doing—we were fighting for ground in a swing state that had been tied most of the 2016 election season—but we also found ways to remind ourselves of the world outside this tiny sphere of seriousness.

Elections and campaigns and politics and the entire culture that builds up around them are at once absolutely ridiculous and incredibly meaningful. I've written articles about things that seemed gigantic at the time but in retrospect were pretty meaningless in the grand scheme. Whether or not Donald Trump sniffed too much in a debate is not a microcosmic indication of larger double standards in debate styles and politics—it's an indication that Trump doesn't understand that microphones in professional settings pick up a lot of noises we don't want them to. But living and working in situations in which a side comment or a sly remark could quickly become the next day's national headline, it becomes harder and harder to step back and understand that life balance. Everything is perfect at all times or it is on fire. There is no in between.

Three weeks before the election, I sat in a coffee shop in Oskaloosa, Iowa, eating my usual chicken ranch sandwich and doing my lunch break reading of Twitter and complaining about my volunteers over texts with a coworker who was also having trouble. And I realized that the essential quandary and pressure of the job was precisely the same quandary that feminist activist work has fallen into over the past few years: we make the perfect the enemy of the good, and in striving to be perfect, we have despised and disregarded the good of things. My volunteers showed up to knock on doors. This is a good thing. They may not have been the most neatly organized or smoothest-run group of canvassers. That's imperfect. But instead of saying "Okay, it's good that we have X, Y, and Z happening," my job as an organizer, and my life as a feminist critic, had trained me to make a list of "shit that went sideways" and set myself with a determination to correct the errors—because they weren't perfect, because I wasn't going to get applause from my boss for how things went, because the standard to which I held myself and to which I was being held were out of sync with what was realistically possible.

And I realized, in that moment: holy buckets, I am Leslie Knope.

For seven years, the popular NBC sitcom *Parks and Recreation* dominated the airwaves, with a documentary style of filming that turned local government into comedy gold. But as any television critic will say, it was comedy with a massive beating heart of gold in the character of Leslie Knope, portrayed by Amy Poehler.

Knope is an optimistic fool in a lot of ways. At the start of the series, she's awkward, intimidating, and enthusiastic about her job to a fault. She's working in local government. She's the deputy director of the parks department in Pawnee, Indiana, a small town where everyone knows each other and the raccoon problem is the stuff of legends. Leslie harbors ambitions that go beyond someone of her particular station. She surrounds herself with pictures of her female heroes—women who served in government for years and who were praised for how well they did their jobs. Hillary Clinton features prominently, as well as Janet Reno and Madeline Albright. When Barack Obama became president, Michelle joined the crew.

Knope is an unabashed feminist, speaking out for women throughout her time in government. She treasures the work of women, praises women roundly, and frequently embarks on campaigns to prove that women are just as capable as men. In one episode, she takes on a job in sanitation to prove to the male sanitation workers that women can and should be hired to do these jobs.

Despite characterizations of feminists as angry women, harpies, and women who have turned bitter after years of rejection, Leslie Knope manages to be a media representation of a feminist who never loses her joy. It is only with the direst of interpretations that Leslie Knope can be turned into a "bitch" of a woman, the slur so frequently hurled at feminists that we named a magazine after it.

But as you can probably guess, feminists still figured out a way to rain on Leslie Knope's joy. Amanda Marcotte, established feminist writer at the *American Prospect*, wrote in 2012 that the decisions made with Leslie Knope's character kneecapped her feminism and forced her into a more traditional role of being "rescued" by her love interest:

> When Leslie, who once swiftly dumped a boyfriend to keep the job she had, finds herself unable to break up with this new boyfriend to get the job she always wanted, Ben saves her by dumping her first. Ben also comes to the rescue when their relationship is revealed to their boss; he quits so that Leslie doesn't lose her job. Ben immediately goes to work as Leslie's campaign manager, because by this point in the show, it's just assumed that he's her natural caretaker.[1]

That reads like interesting, intriguing feminist analysis: except it's a slant reading of the story the show is actually telling. In the name of doing a "feminist" reading and problematizing everyone's favorite TV feminist, Marcotte ends up willfully ignoring basic plot points to get her way. This exemplifies the worst of feminist criticism—refusing to take the art as a whole and instead splicing it into tiny pieces that can be read as "nonfeminist" for the purposes of a hit piece. And this happened again and again with Knope, in part because she was so damn irrepressibly happy.

What actually happens in that season is known as character development. Leslie's major flaw is her thinking that she can do anything and everything all on her own. She depends on her friends, yes, but she's convinced that she, as a feminist, as a woman, can be powerful all on her own and get things achieved by just steamrolling others. This isn't necessarily a bad thing—big personalities are important, but for Leslie, a character who wants to be a good person and values what other people think of her, she has to learn and grow into considering other people's feelings along with her own. It's a basic part of living in common humanity with others and it's essential to her character development. It's why Leslie Knope is endearing, while Michael Scott on *The Office* is grating.

The importance of character, the importance of telling stories, is that we may learn universal human truths from them. A feminist critique that disallows for personal growth is one that denies the sheer power of art. I grew into feminism. I grew into and out of black-and-white thinking. And I can continue to grow *as a feminist*. Feminist art isn't a stopping point—it is about development, about learning how to apply the principles we hold into lessons in the real world. It's about praxis as much as it is about ideology. Which is why it's important that Leslie learns how to love, learns how to maintain her relationships, and, yes, learns how to temper herself without losing herself. This is deeply and vitally important to who Leslie Knope is. And her relationship with Ben—that these critics find problematic—is a major part of that.

Leslie and Ben are actually one of the best examples of a couple that is mutually equal, good for each other, and genuinely loving. And what's more, Leslie remains the star while Ben is her support—he takes on the traditional female role in supporting and campaigning for his politician partner, reflecting a pushback against typical images of a political spouse. They demonstrate funny, if slightly unhealthy ways to manage conflict (Leslie does tackle him at one point to keep him from submitting a negative campaign ad to be aired). And they're genuine friends with chemistry, which makes them work as characters in a relationship.

What's most important, though, is that Leslie never loses her joy, never stops finding ways to look at the world through a happy lens. She is optimistic and sometimes unrealistic to a fault, but even when things are hard, she finds a way to be joyful in a way that reads as *honest*. Developing and cultivating this honest joy is likely what makes her hard to swallow as a feminist figure—she goes against every modern stereotype of a feminist as a serious, practically humorless woman. These are stereotypes we feminists have ourselves fought, but we sometimes find ourselves buying into them when confronted with a character like Leslie Knope. She's our feminist superhero, but could she just be a little less dense about certain things and a little less eternally optimistic?

Unlike her contemporaneous feminist friend Liz Lemon, Leslie Knope isn't cynical; she doesn't think the world exists to take her sandwiches away and make everything suck. She doesn't necessarily greet a new boss and a new situation with fear and dread and put up boundaries. When challenged on her feminism, she tries hard, and snark doesn't sound right coming out of her mouth (which is why it's hilarious when she tries).

Part of the reason Leslie Knope is so refreshing as a character is because she refutes media stereotypes of what a feminist can or should be. Feminist characters have been characterized as frumpy, struggling, humorless bitches unable to laugh at themselves. "Feminist" as a character trait often means deadly serious and unabashedly ambitious. And if they are *funny*? They are somehow betraying some deep feminist understanding of their selfhood. Even Tina Fey's Liz Lemon fell into the frumpy, sex-hating, anxiety-ridden female stereotype by the conclusion of the show.

For a feminist to take on the project of being absolutely, utterly *joyful* is a risky proposition, any way it's sliced.

This is why it's so vitally important that we have Leslie Knope, who validates and justifies every moment when a woman feels wrong for expressing emotion. She is open about her expressions, embraces joy fully, and is unafraid to be angry at the same time.

I'm reminded of an anecdote that Amy Poehler's friend Tina Fey likes to tell about their time on *Saturday Night Live*, where they were both writers and actors for a time. They were sitting around thinking of sketches, and Amy did an impression or a joke that was off-color and involved bodily function. Newer costar Jimmy Fallon, who now has his own late-night talk show, commented through laughter: "Stop that! It's not cute! I don't like it!" And with a quick turn, Amy growled at him, "I don't fucking care if you like it."[2]

One of the aspects of feminist theory that's impossibly hard to pin down is the feminist position on "tone." When I first began writing about feminist issues, I received a plethora of messages from well-meaning male friends giving me instructions on how I must better temper my work and my tone in an effort to win over more people. These messages, though meant in a spirit of helpfulness, ended up instructing me how to do my own job, which only angered me because it assumed a few things: (1) that I was looking for advice on how to win men over to my side, (2) that I was writing for men in the first place, (3) that I needed someone to help me explain and understand what I was doing wrong, (4) that my "tone" was at all angry or contentious to begin with, and (5) that this tone was the problem.

Tone arguments are a method of policing female bodies and our emotions further—they are a reassertion of male dominance in that the work of the oppressed should be in attempting to appeal to their oppressors. Don't rock the boat; be happy and joyful and develop a conciliatory and irenic tone that will help others see your side. We saw this play out in the 2016 election, where, if Hillary smiled, she was questioned about whether or not she was taking issues seriously, and when she didn't, she was accused by Reince Priebus, then head of the Republican National Committee and later Trump's first White House chief of staff, of being dour and not smiling enough.[3] She had to be *perfect* in how she responded to blustering and angry White Man Trump, who interrupted her at twice the rate she did him during the presidential debates, and at one point accused her of being "such a nasty woman."[4]

Our world is littered with implicit and explicit attempts at emotional control of the work that feminists do. As a result, we have a confused idea about what our tone should sound like, to the point where if you *don't* come across as angry and annoyed, you might be doing a bad job of your feminism because no one's correcting your tone—if you aren't making someone angry, you're not a good feminist. We women are in a bind where we are expected to present both an angry "bitch face" to the world and a happy smiling one as women. We can't win in any form.

But what Leslie Knope teaches us is that it's possible to maintain a joyful outlook and become angry when necessary. Knope, as a character and a human being, isn't allowed to simply steamroll over everyone else, which is sometimes the result of feminist critique of the emotional labor women have to go through. She is not the continually angry, performative feminist, but one with complications and joy and sadness and complex relationships with other people. It's hard for her to figure out what she wants her emotional life to be, and she has to have some real, hard conversations with her friends about her tendency to roll right over the emotions of others. In being the woman who wants to win everything and become powerful, she swings too far to one side and actively ignores the feelings and emotions of all others. In one particularly humorous and poignant exchange with her best friend Ann (played by Rashida Jones), Ann points out that Leslie needs to stop steamrolling over people.

LESLIE: Everything is going wrong right now. Whose fault is this? I demand to know!

ANN: Actually, Leslie—

LESLIE: Ben thinks that I'm a steamroller! That's unbelievable. How dare he think that I'm a steamroller.

ANN: Leslie, I'm just telling you this because I love y—

LESLIE: He's just going through a phase right now and eventually we're gonna both be friends again.

ANN: No. What I was really gonna say is that you really are—

LESLIE: —working too hard, I know. Ann, you keep starting all these sentences and not finishing them—

ANN: You're a steamroller. You are a massive! Enormous! Runaway steamroller with no brakes and a cement brick on the gas pedal. You made me watch all eight Harry Potter movies. I don't even *like* Harry Potter.

LESLIE: That's insane! You love Harry Potter. You've seen all eight movies!

ANN: When we go out to a bar, you order my drink for me.

LESLIE: Because you order white wine and it gives you a headache.

ANN: Well it's my headache! Leslie, you do what you want, you ignore what other people want, and you hear only what you wanna hear.[5]

This "come to Jesus" conversation is exactly what is needed for character development. Rather than reining in her feminist tendencies, her friends are urging her to pay attention to other people when she's fulfilling her plans. It's important to her and to them that she takes their thoughts and feelings into account as well. This isn't them suppressing her as a woman and asking her to perform emotional labor for them—this is them begging her to share the burden of the emotional labor everyone has been performing for her.

Leslie's ability to learn and temper herself when she has hurt others is important, realistic engagement of a feminist ethic. These are real conversations real people need to have—it is deeply and desperately important that we learn to deal with and understand each other's emotions and feelings and learn to *share* the division of emotional labor that is part and parcel of engaging with each other in relationship. It is *human*, and that's often totally unexpected in popular culture analysis.

The ultimate result of academic feminist theory when applied critically to popular culture is an imbalance that lacks accounting for real, human emotion. In what can only be described as a poorly thought-out rant on *Splice Today*, Booker Smith called the act of popular culture criticism "intellectual masturbation" and dismissed it altogether. But within the mess, Smith did have one shining, truthful observation: "This recent trend courts two opposing impulses, though: to embrace, and justify, your sincere passions; and to dissect every piece of media, including those idolatrous think pieces, until its problematic roots are exposed. You think *Gilmore Girls* is so important? Well, it actually encourages racism, homophobia, and fat-shaming. Some overeducated English major will probably fire back that criticizing *Gilmore Girls* is a vicious example of taste-shaming. And the cycle will repeat."[6]

Smith is right—we at once do critical analysis to death, robbing the act of watching and spectatorship of any joy it may have once contained, and attempt to justify our selfish tastes as critically fine. But Smith's conclusion from that problem seems to be that we should simply give up the act of criticism altogether, instead of learning to temper ourselves and develop a nuanced approach to our world and the entertainment we create and consume. These choices are not our only options. We are not confined to overzealousness or total apathy. We are capable, like Leslie Knope, of realizing that our zealous joy and passion have a place and need to be tempered with a sense of empathy and understanding. We could realize that at times our criticism needs to go deeper, and at others, our criticism can slow down a bit. It is also necessary to recognize that our anger can move mountains, as Leslie Knope with a fire under her moves an entire bureaucracy to act on the unfair and the unjust.

Knope is a distinctly untempered personality who slowly learns that being human means slowing down sometimes and thinking about others. But—and this is vitally important for who she is as a human, realistic, female character—it doesn't mean giving up on who you are, on what your dreams are, and what you want your life to be. Knope is a distinctly positive figure—the epitome of joy unconstrained and outrage and anger unbounded. And this is an ultimate good, to see both anger and joy held in tension.

One particular episode in the *Parks and Rec* run highlights this tension hilariously. Leslie and Ben, both immense nerds, are in charge of running a Model UN event for the local high schools. Both as a couple who just broke up and as the highly competitive nerdy pair they are, they end up butting heads in front of the entire body of high school students. Leslie ends up shouting at Ben: "The only thing I will be waving is your decapitated head on a stick in front of your weeping mother!"[7] Everything stops as there is a slow dawning realization that she has just gone way too far. Leslie is normally happy, if not controlled, and here, we see the other side of that raw emotion; and, yeah, while yelling what she did at her ex-boyfriend in front of a bunch of high school students wasn't exactly appropriate, it was a great performance of unbounded emotional exercise. This kind of emotional outburst is one frequently banned from women altogether.

Again: character development. The show acknowledges that this outburst, while memorable, and kind of funny, and ultimately real, is something that should give Leslie pause, that should cause her to think back over her actions and wonder why and how she got to that place. Leslie contains the multitudes that are in all of us and creates entertainment out of them while also being a realistic human being. This, ultimately, is Leslie Knope's feminist achievement. She is a female character, on a show surrounded by female characters, who actually manages to live and grow and *exist* as a well-rounded human being, one who changes over time and figures out what works and what doesn't in her situation.

Feminists can learn some important lessons from Ms. Knope: mainly that you are allowed to be who you are, and you can let other people change you without changing the essentials of who you are as a person. You can develop—you don't have to stay stuck at the same loop of feminist criticism so many of us get stuck in, where we are trying every day to be the perfect, unproblematic feminist. That's not who we are. That's not who you are. Let yourself feel joy and anger and everything, and express that. But also let yourself be changed by what you encounter and be that. This is who and what you are.

And if someone calls you on it, you can also just take your inspiration from Leslie: "I guess some people just object to powerful depictions of awesome ladies."[8]

13

Teen Girls Are the Future and
That Is a Good Thing

Our Perfectionism Actively Harms Women

Sometime in 2016 there was a shift in the world of journalism. Mainstream media and traditional journalism outlets began losing the analysis game—people were looking beyond the papers of record to get thoughts and political opinions. Now, mainstream newspapers did a lot of brilliant work throughout the course of the election, but many places dropped the ball. The balance of coverage shifted in very specific ways as traditional journalists tried to take a "both sides" stance on what ultimately was a very strange political year. Threats to access on the campaign trail caused several news organizations to become timid. In the most flagrant example, America's newspaper of record, the *New York Times*, elected not to publish explosive allegations that the Trump campaign had communicated with the Kremlin about the 2015–16 hacking attacks on the Democratic National Committee. Nearly all of these allegations later proved to be true—there was a dossier detailing a relationship between Russia and the Trump camp, and the FBI requested a special warrant from the Justice Department to investigate. As of this writing, the story has continued into the second year of Trump's presidency, with more allegations about contact between the Trump campaign and Russia being confirmed as true. But all this came out after Trump had been elected. The Gray Lady had been "too timid" (in the words of one of their editors) to move forward with the story.[1]

The year 2016 changed the quality and understanding of journalism and political analysis. The Trump campaign (and later the Trump administration) exhibited an incredible hostility to the press, with Trump himself calling the media "the opposition party."[2] Outlets pulled back on their criticism of him for fear of being banned from his campaign events. So outlets that were not well known for their journalistic efforts stepped in to fill the gap. *Teen Vogue* stepped up. *Cosmopolitan* stepped up. *Rolling Stone* stepped up. These "pop culture" outlets became indispensable in their cutting analysis and political heft.

In early June 2016, a man walked into a nightclub in Orlando, Florida, and opened fire. He killed forty-nine people, and then himself, in what was at that time, the deadliest mass shooting in recent American history. I was in England, finishing up my dissertation, and my queer friends and I gathered with over five hundred fellow LGBT citizens at the library in the center of town for a large vigil. Candles were set around the famous library with the names of each of the victims.

Within hours of the news breaking, editors were pulling together articles about any related issues and angle they could think of. This wasn't some morbid method of increasing clicks, but rather an attempt to get the information out there and do the best job they could in helping others find the best information and analysis quickly. I got an email from a friend who is also a freelance writer asking if I could fill in for her on an op-ed that one of her regular outlets needed.

And that's how I ended up writing for *Cosmopolitan* magazine. I hurriedly put together analysis of the Federal Drug Administration's continued ban on blood donations from men who sleep with men—a rule that seemed particularly harsh following the death of so many queer men. After a little back and forth with the editor, the article was up and out to the world. When I posted it on my social media channels, I got a consistent reply that made me roll my eyes every time someone said it: "Wait, *Cosmo* does analysis like that?"

Yes, *Cosmo*, the magazine known for ridiculous sex tips and articles about new antiaging methods was, in fact, engaged in some deeply important political analysis. My friend Robin Marty, who had gotten me the gig, had been covering reproductive rights for the magazine for ages. They also had a beat on presidential politics and a vertical on gay and lesbian issues. A magazine aimed at women, covering actual politics? Shocking.

Back when I first started writing professionally, I did a few pieces for the Christian magazine RELEVANT. More accurately, I did two pieces and got every pitch after that rejected because it was too political, and then I just gave up. A year later, in a broader fight about women's issues coverage in Christian media, I did a data analysis of the vertical that I'd contributed to at RELEVANT. And I discovered a troubling pattern: stories on current events and politics were almost entirely written by men. Stories on relationships, marriage, and the like were almost entirely by women. There was, at the time, a clear delineation between who could contribute what to which conversation. And it was clear that women were not to comment on actual political issues that affected their daily lives—that was left for the men.

The shock that women would want to have a part in political discussions and analysis feels like a leftover from the Victorian era. No reasonable person would agree outright with the statement that "women shouldn't read politics." But framed slightly different, and their shock and surprise betrays a deeper-rooted misogyny: "*Teen Vogue* is doing some of the best political coverage of our time."

The tweets roll in:

So now @TeenVogue is the paper that goes after real stories in this country. 2016 is some kind of fucked up, amirite?[3]

Ya'll @TeenVogue is protecting democracy better than most any other publication/media outlet, they may win a Pulitzer. Real #Journalism.[4]

Wow, Teen Vogue? I'm going to subscribe to TEENVOGUE??? http://www.teenvogue.com/story/donald-trump-is-gaslighting -america ... via @TeenVogue.[5]

@wstafrican @talktoskirt Who thought Teen Vogue would be the only upstanding news outlet in America these days.[6]

The savior of journalism right now is literally Teen Vogue. Not even joking.[7]

Teen Vogue published this.

Teen Vogue!

TEENVOGUE!!!![8]

Doing a better job of explaining #Trump & what he did than most veteran #journalists. @TeenVogue—#gaslighting.[9]

That was in a two-minute search on a random Saturday afternoon in late 2016, shortly after *Teen Vogue* released an article of solid analysis, criticizing then President-elect Donald Trump as a gaslighting abuser. The condescension is almost palpable: "OMGTEEN-VOGUEISDOINGIMPORTANTSTUFF," as though women's magazines are incapable of doing anything besides talking about how green is the color for spring this year. Even among "good" liberal folk, there's still an air of condescension and surprise when teenage girls prove themselves capable of engagement and thought. For the most part, we don't doubt that a fifteen-year-old in Texas can build a clock by himself, but we're shocked and surprised when a magazine aimed at teenage girls comes out with unique analysis that "veteran journalists" didn't think of. This shock and surprise extends out of a cultural condescension toward teen girls in general.

One particularly memorable incident of condescension toward teen readers and those who write for them occurred on December 23, 2016, on Tucker Carlson's Fox News program *Tucker Carlson Tonight*. After *Teen Vogue* published an important article on how Trump is gaslighting America, the author, Lauren Duca, caught the eye of major news networks—both friendly and unfriendly. Her Twitter came under scrutiny, and after Ivanka Trump was confronted publicly on an airplane over support for her father, Carlson had Duca on to discuss the incident.

But Carlson refused to stay on that topic. About halfway through, he switched topics to discussing Duca's work. And the result was an astounding mess.

CARLSON: You wrote this piece in *Teen Vogue*, which I guess you write for.

DUCA: Oh, which you guess I write for? Yes, that's not fake news, that's real news. You *guess*? Oh, you guess? You guess, Tucker? That's really patronizing.

CARLSON: Well I've never read *Teen Vogue* because I'm not a *Teen Vogue* reader . . .

DUCA: . . . So did you read the entire article?

CARLSON: I did! I also read "Liam Payne is 100% Certain One Direction Will Continue," "Arianna Grande Rocked the Most Epic Thigh-High Boots at Jingle Bell" and—

DUCA: Yes, it's incredible.

CARLSON: [unintelligible] "Went through the Messiest Break-Up of 2016." Those are your other pieces. But I'm trying to get to what you're writing about Trump, taking a break from the thigh-high boots and ask what you mean about him committing psychological abuse on you.

DUCA: Women can love Arianna Grande and her thigh-high boots and—

CARLSON: (laughing) Okay, I'm just—

DUCA: Talk about politics and those things are not mutually exclusive. Now that you bring up *Teen Vogue*, we— we treat young women like they don't have a right to a political conversation—

CARLSON:—to a bunch of dumb propaganda!

[Duca and Carlson talk over each other unintelligibly]

DUCA: And those things are not mutually exclusive, so you know what? I did write about Arianna Grande and I did write about the abusive, bigoted—

CARLSON: Those pieces are a little smarter than your piece about threatening the sovereignty of a whole religion. Alright, I gotta go. Lauren, you should stick to the thigh-high boots. You're better at that.

DUCA: [as her mic is being cut off]: You're a sexist pig.

The condescension toward the complicated life of teenage girls—and the condescension toward the things they care about—is palpable throughout the conversation. An article's appearance alongside articles about celebrities in a magazine written for teen girls is reason enough to dismiss it, regardless of quality of content or insight.

A major reason behind the rejection of much of popular culture is a not-so-subtle sexism toward women—young women in particular. We are considered naïve, uneducated, shallow. What we do is devalued precisely because of our participation in it. This, I contend, is the motivation behind the devaluation of popular culture studies in the academic sphere and the devaluation of popular culture journalism in the mainstream sphere. I've run into both in the course of my professional life, carving out a niche of popular culture criticism within "lowbrow" artistic ventures. Just because it appears on the CW Network doesn't mean it's automatically discounted. And just because it's on HBO doesn't mean it's a prestige piece.

In addition to these extant problems with what we deem high or low culture, the dismissive attitude toward aspects of popular culture tends to fall along the lines of what is enjoyed by women versus what has a larger audience among men. Think Batman versus Wonder Woman. Think Lord of the Rings versus Dragonriders of Pern. Think Sam Smith versus Taylor Swift. It's common for something that is incredibly similar in tone and subject matter to be received better if it comes from a man—and this principle isn't just true of business meetings or classroom biases. It's true of how we treat popular culture in general.

This principle—that media created by and for women is to be devalued—isn't constrained to how bros view popular culture, but includes how feminists themselves see and critique popular culture. It is important, I believe, for us to examine carefully our own biases toward female artists. Are we rejecting Katy Perry because we genuinely think her music is bad, or are we rejecting her because her popularity stems from being beloved by teenage girls? This is particularly relevant when we move into the territory of rejecting female celebrities for paper-thin reasons. For this case study, I give you Anne Hathaway.

I've loved Anne Hathaway ever since she broke onto the scene in 2001's *The Princess Diaries*. The story, brilliantly told and acted, was one full of antifeminist tropes: young woman is informed she is actually a princess of a country she's never heard of and must be reformed into a Lady. Everything that makes her herself is wiped away in a classical transformation montage: her teeth are straightened, her hair is straightened, her back is straightened. She becomes the princess, gets back at the haters in her school, and gets the guy. For fifteen-year-old me, alone and dateless in high school, this movie was a dream.

And then the backlash started.

People hated Anne Hathaway. "You fucking suck." "Fuck Anne Hathaway. That bitch ruins everything." "Talentless actress. Baggy-eyed. Generally sad sack." "Anne Hathaway is a boring person. I hate boring people." "Huge horse mouth."[10]

Anne Hathaway, despite starring in some of the biggest movies in recent years—*The Devil Wears Prada, Love and Other Drugs, Les Miserables*—became the target of unfiltered and unabashed hatred. People hated how she looked, how she dressed, how she acted, how she didn't act. She literally could not make a move that didn't upset someone. All this hatred seemed to stem from the fact that she was beloved first and foremost by teenage girls. She'd gotten her start in a particularly saccharine movie marketed directly at teenage girls, fulfilling the fantasy that they could secretly be princesses. When she followed up that success with *The Devil Wears Prada*, a movie where she plays the frumpy assistant to Meryl Streep's demanding and incisive fashion magazine editor, it seemed to cement her as the girl who played "soft" roles, who catered to teen girls, and who cared about what teen girls thought.

It was this last, ultimately, that did her in. She was unabashedly a hero to teenage girls, someone who loved being in movies aimed at them, and who seemed very approachable and loving. She was a suitable role model for them as well—when paparazzi published photos of her having a wardrobe malfunction while getting out of a car, her response was to point out that paparazzi selling that photo were participating in the commodification of another person's sexuality and failing to be decent people. And this, to a lot of people, is enraging—because she's a woman who refuses to take any crap, who is a good role model for teenagers, and who prizes the work of women and girls.

But what is also enraging, as other astute writers have noted, is her seemingly unending supply of toothy grins and ready laughs. She is an unabashedly happy woman who lets others see that she is happy. And that, simply, cannot stand, for a lot of people.

Anne Helen Peterson summed up the problem in a feature for BuzzFeed:

Which is part of the problem, of course: You can't calculate charisma or cool. Both are contingent on the absence of trying, and Anne Hathaway is nothing if not a woman-shaped aggregation of trying. All female celebrities, like all people, are of course trying at something; it's just that some, like [Jennifer] Lawrence, do a (much) better job of hiding the effort. And stardom, like so much of the contemporary manufacture of the self vis-à-vis the internet, is rooted in final products that betray no signs of labor.[11]

The so-called Anne Hathaway Syndrome is an example of how women—and teenage girls—are expected to try without looking like they're trying. Your skin and makeup and hair need to be flawless, and you can't look like you've tried to look that way or you're "unnatural." This, even as we understand that a "natural" makeup look takes a long time to perfect. "Great" hair takes a lot of time in a stylist's chair or working with it in the mirror in the mornings. Perfection doesn't happen without effort, and when we praise effortlessness, we cannot therefore expect perfection.

This, too, is seen in the backlash against various female celebrities as they attempt to maintain their "cool girl" vibe that once captivated audiences. Somewhere around the time she won an Oscar, Jennifer Lawrence moved from "Hollywood Cool Girl" to "Girl Who Tries Too Hard to Seem Cool." Natalie Portman went the same direction after the Thor movies. And Anna Kendrick lost it around the time she wrote a book about it. Mindy Kaling had it for a moment before a white TV audience realized that brown girls are never the Cool Girl.

Slasher fiction author Gillian Flynn summed up the issue succinctly (and ironically?) in *Gone Girl*:

Men always say that as the defining compliment, don't they? She's a cool girl. Being the Cool Girl means I am a hot, brilliant, funny woman who adores football, poker, dirty jokes, and burping, who plays video games, drinks cheap beer, loves threesomes and anal sex, and jams hot dogs and hamburgers into her mouth like she's hosting the world's biggest culinary gang bang while somehow maintaining a size 2, because Cool Girls are above all hot. Hot and understanding. Cool Girls never get angry; they only smile in a chagrined, loving manner and let their men do whatever they want. Go ahead, shit on me, I don't mind, I'm the Cool Girl.[12]

Countless teenage girls lose hours and days of time trying hard to be the Cool Girl, to fit in perfectly in whatever way they're expected to. Furthermore, if their effort to be this prototype of a girl is visible, everything they wanted to achieve is useless. They're already fighting an uphill battle in trying to become exactly what the world wants them to be—and they're doing it in the face of messaging that says their opinions, their ideas, their humanness is useless and unworthy and silly and ridiculous.

If you're not admiring teenage girls for putting up with all of that, I don't know where your head is.

And that, ultimately, is what we need to keep in mind with every bit of popular culture criticism we engage in and the work we do: are we rejecting something on its own merits or are we looking at it more harshly because it's popular with teenage girls? Where is our motivation to pathologize and categorize and dismiss certain areas or levels of popular culture coming from?

These are the questions we have to ask ourselves every time we put fingers to keys to write a piece of criticism or think piece about popular culture. A hot take isn't enough—we have to dig deeper and recognize our own biases and ingrained problems as we move forward. Before we declare something problematic, we must look at how often we are declaring things teen girls love as unworthy.

One of the best ways to check ourselves is to actually *listen* to the things teenage girls are doing and saying and consuming. Subscribe to *Teen Vogue*. Read *The Rookie*. Read young adult lit. Get plugged back into what teen girls are consuming and buying and thinking.

After all, teen girls are a *massive* market demographic in this late-stage capitalist era we live in. To not pay attention to what teen girls are doing and saying is foolish, especially for people who make a living as culture critics.

Being a teen girl is not a pathology. It's not a disease that will make you less respectable or make your opinions less valid. It is, however, a unique position in the world in which you are developing an understanding and approach to a world that hates you. Being able to hold onto your opinions and your ideas without compromise in the fact of that kind of onslaught takes guts and it takes work. This is why teenage girls are, to me, the demographic most deserving of our respect, as human beings and cultural critics.

14

Never Say Never

Setting Your Own Borders and
Understanding Your Boundaries

There's a bar I know of that was usually a stop on a night of bad decisions. A touristy burger joint by day and a seedy club by night, this bar was up a flight of stairs above the main street. It was the place of legends: this was where Katy lost her sub fusc (school uniform) and went home with two guys at the same time. This was where the bartender sneaked some alcohol into a "shot" of Coca-Cola my friend had gotten me (I don't drink). And this was where the loud, drunk, body-builder Russian dude got himself kicked out and all of us were grateful that the UK has very strict gun laws because he looked just mad and drunk enough to do something.

This bar also had terrible music, blasting too loudly for anyone to hear themselves. I was always the sober one in the group, so I was always completely cognizant of just how terrible the selection was. My friends, usually several drinks in by the time we ended up there, just cared that it had a beat and that they could move. Occasionally one of them would snap back to reality and realize what we were actually dancing to.

One night in January, my friend Kyle had this waking-up moment as the familiar "hey hey hey errybody get up" of Robin Thicke's controversial and much criticized "Blurred Lines" blasted over the speakers. As Thicke's falsetto enveloped the club, Kyle froze in place, put his head down and threw his hands up in the air, giving a one fingered salute to the DJ. The song didn't suddenly change or stop, but he held his spot in the middle of the dance floor for almost the entire song. The rest of us burst out laughing and pulled out our phones to take a picture of this tiny protest, and then returned to dancing. Walking off the floor wasn't going to change the DJ's selection—our nights out had demonstrated as much. Whether it was a bop hosted by another college or a nightclub in the city, the reaction of the people on the dance floor seemed to have little effect on the music that was actually played.

As critics who are also consumers of media, this can make a person feel incredibly small. We have no power over what's happening, and we can't really dictate what becomes popular. In this late-capitalist stage, we are simply one part of a much larger machine of popular music churned out and played for us. Our individual choices as consumers don't feel like they have a huge impact, so our protests and our criticisms and our middle fingers are all part of expressing both powerlessness at the capitalist machine and our own displeasure with what we hear, see, and consume. Sometimes it's all we have.

Perhaps that's cynical of me. After all, I just spent a lot of words and a lot of chapters explaining exactly how we can become better consumers of our media and how we can respond to those outside influences that tell us there are certain virtues in our small protests and criticisms. There is also power in the collective group that threatens action based on a critical displeasure with the status quo. Collective action is what changes the world. But collective action with regard to cultural phenomena is often slippery and hard to grasp. Are people actively boycotting or is the show just unpopular? Is there a difference? How do we get showrunners and popular artists to listen? The protests become as much about individual action as about the object being critiqued, and fall apart.

This becomes even harder when matters of personal taste are turned into matters of communal virtue. You can't see *Dr. Strange* because it's a whitewashing movie and we can't support that in Hollywood. You can't listen to Kanye West because he called Taylor Swift a bitch. Or you should listen to Kanye because Taylor Swift *is* being an underhanded bitch to him. You shouldn't go to movies starring Christian Bale, Sean Penn, Casey Affleck, Mickey Rourke, Johnny Depp, Christian Slater, Charlie Sheen, Adrien Brody, Michael Fassbender, or Josh Brolin. You must cleanse yourself and your art of any remnant of potential antiwoman or antifeminist thought.

But as the philosopher Justin Bieber once said, "Never say never."

In an ideal world, no person who has engaged in abuse would have a public-facing career where people would look up to them. But the fact of the matter is that we don't live in an ideal world, and this method of "boycott their work" once you find out that they have engaged in abusive behavior is unsustainable. Every day, the list of "nope, never" grows larger and the list of permissible entertainment shrinks. Something's gonna break, and, I contend, something already has.

Feminism can't happen through creating lists of permissible and impermissible media. We've been trying that for years, and it hasn't worked. There has been slow, plodding change, to be sure, but the cultural sea change that was supposed to develop from our boycotts and our fierce criticisms hasn't come into being. Labeling everything "problematic" has essentially rendered the term useless—we relied on it to do all of our critical thinking for us and acted surprised when it became a joke. Aiming for perfection has caused us to ignore the good that can be contributed through art.

One of my favorite movies from 2002 is *The Pianist*. It tells the true-life story of Wladysaw Szpilman, a Jewish pianist in Warsaw who escaped the Nazis and survived by hiding in a bombed-out ghetto for months. The movie stars Adrien Brody as Szpilman, in a performance that eventually earned him an Academy Award for Best Actor. The movie was directed by Roman Polanski, a man who fled the United States in the late 1970s after a plea bargain for a charge of statutory rape fell through and he realized he would be jailed beyond the forty-two days he'd already served. Since then he has been living abroad, as both Poland and Switzerland have rejected extradition requests on him from the United States. Many Hollywood actors (both men and women) have signed petitions requesting that the charges be dropped and Polanski be allowed to return to the United States, a place he had made his home for so many years.

The details of the case are harrowing. In 1977 Polanski requested that he be allowed to photograph a thirteen-year-old girl for an edition of *Vogue* he was guest editing. He arranged a private photo shoot with the girl and proceeded to give her a partial dose of quaaludes and some champagne. After she was drugged, he assaulted and raped her, both vaginally and anally, with his victim telling him to stop at every opportunity. After this was reported to the police, Polanski was arrested and charged with rape by use of drugs, perversion, sodomy, lewd and lascivious acts upon a child under fourteen, and furnishing a controlled substance to a minor. He pled down to a charge of unlawful intercourse with a minor, but fled the country hours before his sentencing because he feared he would be either imprisoned or deported.

Polanski, to this day, denies that the sex—which neither party disputes having occurred—was nonconsensual. He has insisted so in writing, and throughout interviews. Polanski was forty-four years old at the time and a powerful artist in the industry, having made the incredibly popular and critically acclaimed *Chinatown* just a few years prior. He had promised his victim a photo spread in *Vogue*, which he did not deliver, and had used his power to encourage her—a thirteen-year-old child—to pose topless. His behavior is deeply troubling and disgusting, as a forty-four-year-old has absolutely no business doing private photo shoots with topless thirteen-year-olds, much less engaging in sexual acts with them.

This is the fact of the matter as it stands. As a feminist, as a woman, as a sexual assault survivor, I am loath to give him any room or leniency, especially since he used his considerable resources specifically to avoid prosecution. Many spin the potential jail time and deportation as a change in the existing plea bargain, but the fact of the matter is that Polanski pled guilty and then refused to accept punishment for his crimes, which indicates he was using the guilty plea as a means to escape justice, rather than to confront it.

All of that makes me sick as a feminist.

And yet, I still love *The Pianist*. I adore Brody's performance in the movie, and I find it a harrowing depiction of the terror of the Holocaust, as told by a survivor of the Holocaust (both through the lens of Szpilman's autobiography and Polanski's own experience with the war). It is an important film in the scheme of film studies. It was made by someone who has committed utterly reprehensible acts and refuses to own up to them. Both of these statements are true. These are two truths I must deal with every time I pull up *The Pianist* on my streaming service of choice. Is it possible for me to appreciate the contributions of *Chinatown* and *The Pianist* and his version of *Macbeth* while also understanding and acknowledging that he, as a man, has done terrible things?

Perhaps I am the bad person for continuing to watch Polanski movies when I have the knowledge of his awful deeds. Perhaps I am a hypocrite for rejecting Woody Allen movies for the same reason while continuing to say that film studies needs to teach *Chinatown*. Perhaps I am not a feminist at all.

I have been accused of worse.

This is the dilemma of a feminist who consumes media. And this is my advice: Give yourself permission to recognize the tensions and to understand that your line distinguishing what is acceptable from unacceptable might be different from someone else's when it comes to the art you consume. Do so with the full knowledge that there are many people who will draw the line in a different place than you. I cannot watch Woody Allen movies, because so many of them are autobiographical, and he stars in most of them, imbuing them with his incredibly icky rationalizations about sexuality and age. Allen has been accused, consistently, of molesting his former wife's daughter when she was just a child. He also married his adopted daughter after what many allege were years of grooming her to be compliant. And his movies, especially from around this era, reflect a lot of those totally fucked-up sexual politics.

I cannot enjoy *Manhattan* or *Annie Hall* anymore. Looking at his face makes me sick to my stomach, and I think any teaching of his movies in a classroom setting needs to come with the context of his alleged crimes, as they inform the autobiographical nature of his movies and the choices he makes as a director.

So why do I draw the line where I do? Why can I stand to watch *Chinatown* but not *Annie Hall*? Is it a matter of story versus biography? Is it because, for Woody Allen, the line between film and life is a blurry one, while Polanski seems to demarcate it a little clearer? Perhaps. And perhaps I'm simply developing a method of justification so I can keep watching movies I love without consequence or backlash.

At least, that's what I'll be accused of, because it is impossible to logically justify the consumption of some art but not others. We frequently apply an inflexible "objective" standard to art regardless of its claims to feminism. But maybe in this push to better ourselves, we have forgotten how to talk about art as art and to discuss the contributions each piece makes to its field. We have created our own lists of do's and don't's that are frequently arbitrary and questionable in themselves. We declare a piece problematic and then shame and judge people who continue to engage with it.

This is not to say we should take part in artistic endeavors without consideration of their creators. It is impossible to read Hemingway without awareness of his history as an alcoholic and a womanizer. In a lot of ways, we understand art better when we understand the creator, even as we are repulsed. That repulsion can even be effective, as repulsive artists occasionally go on to hoist themselves with their own petard, placing all of their art within a new context.

Take the Woody Allen revelations, for example. The accusations of pedophilia against Allen caused a major shift in how we read his earlier work, especially his repetitive trope of an older man falling in love with a younger woman. It is an insight into his attempted justification of his behavior, and therefore his art continues to implicate him in his crimes. The allegations also shift film criticism about his work. Where many of his autobiographical works would be seen as somewhat benign, simply telling a weird story, we now see the effect his alleged real-life predilections and predatory behaviors have had and the ways in which he sought to normalize that behavior with his art. It all clicks into place.

This, of course, runs right up against the question of platform versus free speech. We don't have to give artists who have committed crimes a platform, to be sure. But it's arguable that the art we do have should not be ignored and should be engaged with rather than simply rejected out of hand. Hemingway is important for understanding shifts in modern American literature, and his attitudes toward women are an important part of engaging with him, just as Polanski's *Chinatown* is a beast of 1970s cinema and is important for cinema studies.

It would be nice and convenient if terrible people only produced terrible work that we could dismiss. It'd be great if every director/writer/producer were a Michael Bay clone, in that their "art" reflects just how *awful* their personal attitudes toward women are. But that's not the world we live in, and it's impossible to purify any and every piece of entertainment or culture from the taint of abuse. That's the nature of living in a culture of abuse, and we must grapple with what that means for popular culture and for the works we deal with. Are they promoting their criminalist views and attitudes within their work? Or does the art stand apart on its own merit? And what does it mean to develop a critical lens in light of an authorial biography that's terrible?

These are all questions we have to answer if we want to effectively and critically engage with popular culture.

Our own world of feminist theory is not free from the "problematic" label. The world of feminist theory is a mess. In many ways, current theory is attributable to a lot of white, racist feminists. The development of current Western feminism started with the suffragettes in both the UK and the U.S. And these suffragettes were largely racist—there were abolitionist movements that linked up with suffragists, but the movements stayed largely separate. The academic theory and philosophy that developed from white women demanding a position within the white male world of philosophy is what gave us Simone de Beauvoir and, eventually, Judith Butler. The ignorance of the womanist movement in the 1960s and '70s by second-wave feminism resulted in parallel development of theory, with black female theorists engaging with the work of their white, racist counterparts and knocking it down to size. Indeed, Kimberlé Crenshaw's famous discussions about intersectionality extended out of real-world experiences at conferences and in academic settings. Audre Lorde's oft-quoted line, "the master's tools will never dismantle the master's house," appears in an essay roundly criticizing feminist theory conferences as being white-centric.

We wouldn't have feminist theory if Simone de Beauvoir hadn't been in a relationship with the problematic ass Jean Paul Sartre. We wouldn't necessarily be where we are in terms of the development and understanding of feminist and gender theory if we had developed a sense of ideological purity and refused to engage with people like Margaret Sanger, who founded Planned Parenthood and advocated for birth control while also promoting eugenics. We can recognize problematic things in retrospect and regret them—I despise that white feminism rejected womanism and womanist contributions for such an extended period. But I also recognize that without one we wouldn't have the other, and it's a tension-filled position to be in. It's not pure, it's not happy, but it's *real*. It's historical. It's what our theory's development and historical context *is*.

If we decide to engage with feminist theory, we need to understand that it is not ideologically pure. Judith Butler championed some amazing and important changes to the ways in which we view and enact and perform gender, and she said some pretty bad stuff. While Adrienne Rich wrote incredibly important commentary on lesbian existence and compulsory heterosexuality—a term still necessary for a lot of queer theory today—her focus on the lesbian experience ends up being fairly biphobic and therefore problematic. As a bisexual woman, I think there's more to be said and important critiques to be made about Rich's biphobia, and I also believe she's added immensely to my own understanding of my sexuality and to my feminism. She is the author who sparked a lot of my feminist interest to begin with and I owe a great debt to her. Shall I give her up because of the biphobia in one of her landmark essays? Or should I engage with that content, rejecting untruth and embracing truth?

We are now attempting to develop a feminist ethic for approaching popular culture, and unfortunately, that has turned into a hunt for perfect, ideological, purity. It has deemed that anything "problematic" be cast aside as never good enough, not perfect enough. We have built an ethic dependent on never making a wrong step. But to do so is a denial of the real world, and the engagement with some form of artistic endeavor shouldn't stop for everyone because of an aspect deemed problematic.

Roman Polanski is not Adrienne Rich. He is not excluding people while developing solid theory. But Polanski is an important contributor to our understanding of film as it exists today, and we can keep his art within the context in which it was created and take with skepticism any ideas of justice or injustice that he presents in his films. Similarly, our knowledge of Woody Allen radically changes and challenges how we approach his artistic endeavors and what it means to consume his work. As consumers, we get to make the choice about what we want to pay to see, to be sure. But as cultural critics, our job is not to condemn and write off programs that don't align with our political ideology, but to engage and critique them in a way that also exemplifies our ideals.

I grew up in a culture that dictated that we needed to be "in the world but not of it." A conservative, deeply spiritual Christian, I was convinced I should not cast my eyes on anything that did not glorify God and did not further His Kingdom. This meant no Top Forty, no R-Rated movies, no sex scenes or heavy violence, and certainly no swearing. I distinctly remember one time telling my dad I didn't like the Backstreet Boys because in their song "Everybody (Backstreet's Back)," A.J. shouts, "Oh my god we're back again."

"That's taking the Lord's name in vain and I don't like it!" I declared triumphantly. And foolishly.

But the result of my strict purity ideology was that I didn't experience a lot of art that would have been beneficial for me, and when I finally did, it took me a long time to develop the tools to process it. By the time I hit college, I'd loosened up a bit and was embracing more films and literature that was "questionable," at least according to my uptight Christian, black-and-white standard. As it turns out, I learned and grew as a human being by engaging with art I previously found damaging. Perhaps that art did damage me—after all I'm here: the author of a book about sex and another one about popular culture, a bisexual, agnostic on most days, and feminist woman. Perhaps I should have maintained a practice of avoidance, and perhaps that is how feminism should continue to approach culture that is "bad," by an unspoken set of feminist standards. But I don't think that's the route we need to take.

There is a virtual minefield of tests that any person wishing to be a "good feminist" must pass, and many of these are unspoken until you accidentally land on one. Ideally, you'd have enough friends and good people around you to correct your errors and catch them before they become public mistakes, but for many of us who are learning, who are processing, it can be incredibly scary to make a misstep. We don't allow room for enthusiastic support of the problematic popular culture artifact unless there is adequate supplication about what is wrong with it. Our enjoyment of a thing must come with caveats and warnings and discussion of the problematic parts, lest we be seen as uncritically endorsing an object of displeasure for many.

Perhaps we need to start trusting that feminism isn't just something we do publicly. For some reason, we don't trust that people are doing the work without being public about it. Any assertion of public enjoyment without the necessary caveats is viewed with skepticism—to declare, uncritically, that you enjoyed an episode of *Girls* or watched *Dr. Strange* is to erode trust in your ability to think critically. This performative aspect of modern critical thinking has created an atmosphere in which failure to perform correctly, failure to engage in a public manner, means nothing is happening and nothing will happen and you have failed—you cannot say "Hey, I like this song" without also linking to the current definitive argument on the subject.

Right around the time my first book came out, in early 2015, there was a massive hubbub happening online involving one of my book's endorsers and a conference she had scheduled using angel funds from a man many in postevangelical work hated. His ex-wife had accused him of physical and emotional abuse, and my impression of him was such that I was inclined to believe the ex-wife. I saw the mob building after my friend announced the conference, threatening to destroy a woman-focused retreat that would be good for the progressive, post-evangelical church.

My book was due to come out in ten days and I was dealing with a lot of personal crises in addition to this major life event. I emailed my friend—the endorser—and had an extended conversation with her about the problems with working with this man, and we talked about her position within all this and how she felt about all of it. I was thinking about it almost constantly and was torn about what to do.

And then I saw my own work being pulled into this backlash and people surmising that I was conspiring evilly with the conference runners, because apparently there's a lot of money in book endorsements. And I couldn't get away from it. Because I'd not publicly performed the calling-out aspects of the outrage but rather had approached my friend in private, knowing this had a much better chance of making a difference, I was suddenly antifeminist, antiwoman, and pro-abuse. Because I dared to not *perform* my feminism and had instead acted on it away from the public spotlight, I was accused of being in the pocket of the abusers. To this day, people accuse me of failure in feminism, having no idea what work was being done behind the scenes.

This same plague has enveloped feminism as a whole, where a private action is worthless unless a public declaration is then made. "Pics or it didn't happen" has come to feminist criticism. And it has destroyed it.

Last Notes

When Donald Trump won the election to become president of the United States, I wondered, quite seriously, if talking about feminist criticism really was a topic worth discussing. The validation of misogyny, the rise of fascism, the threat on checks and balances presented by the Trump administration—each of these things seemed like reason enough to set aside this project for happier times, times less fraught with people literally fighting for their lives. This brings me to the final necessary discussion of feminist criticism: have we put popular culture in its proper place?

In the days following the 2016 election, as millions of progressives across the nation were mourning both the loss of the first female presidency and the rise of a sexist, racist, xenophobic man to the White House, many turned to fiction. Harry Potter's fight against a creeping, fascistic, autocratic regime turned into a valuable metaphor for understanding current events. Identification with a specific Hogwarts House clarified and motivated many people who grew up reading the books. Reminders of the fight against Voldemort helped many who grew up with the series process a potential role in the new state.

In similar ways, Suzanne Collins's *The Hunger Games* provided metaphorical understanding of how to fight back. Dystopian fiction saw an uptick in sales in the days following Trump's inauguration. *Brave New World*, *1984*, and *The Handmaid's Tale* all began to fly off the shelves again as people sought to understand rebellion and revolution after living so comfortably for so long. Fictional stories seemed to develop a new power, a new understanding, in the midst of a terrifying world.

There's something more going on here than just people looking for an escape hatch from the world of Donald Trump. Fiction gives us the words and the ideas and the positioning to understand ourselves. Fiction gives us space to explore and understand. It gives us heroes to follow and emulate. And it gives us the words to describe and understand the frustration of our experiences. Fiction—and by extension, popular culture—can act as an important tool of political resistance, not just as an escape from the everyday.

But this only works if a person is willing to see it and to think critically about what culture says about our lives now, not just what it said about the time in which it was written. We become Katniss fighting President Snow, Harry fighting both the Ministry of Magic and Lord Voldemort, John Preston discovering how to feel in *Equilibrium*. Popular culture is important because of how it speaks to the heart, both in our political consternation and our theological upheavals. It is a way we can learn to walk in another person's shoes, even if imperfectly or slightly bungled. When we force popular culture to perfectly reflect our ideology before we engage with it, however, when we request perfection before or absent of critical evaluation, we rob ourselves of those chances to see life from another person's eyes.

This doesn't rule out critique as an important method of understanding. But it does place it in its proper position within feminist praxis. Critical thinking on the part of the individual is far more important than feminist perfection in the art we consume. When I speak to my dad about the fake news story he's just read, it's more important to me that he learn how to question the things he reads online than that he agrees with me in this one instance. The learning process, aided by criticism, helps us along in this task. It is a vital partner in implementing a feminist understanding of the world. Criticism cannot replace critical thinking, which is the way the feminist movement has behaved with regard to pop culture in recent years.

In a world where Republicans are voting to destroy health care as we know it, where anti-immigrant xenophobia and jingoism are at extreme heights, and people are becoming more politically engaged than I've seen in my short lifetime, it is deeply important that we embrace critical thinking about what we engage with and what we consume. Critical thinking does not just declare something a problem and boycotts it, but engages, argues, persuades, and understands. It is important to have boundaries. It is more important to be able to engage readily with why those boundaries exist and push ourselves not only to understand the boundary but what it means for our feminist ethic of equity and understanding.

We don't need to read countless think pieces about disappointed Trump voters in order to understand them. But we should consider the voters in our lives, critically engaging with their thoughts and sharpening our own ideas in developing understanding. We do not need to listen to Trump babble about Mar-a-Lago, but we should, at least, pay some attention to what the administration is doing.

And you don't have to listen to rapper Macklemore to develop a nuanced critical opinion that understands his place in the world. You don't have to engage, if that's your position. But you also shouldn't prevent others from attempting to develop their own understanding of the world around them. Harry Potter may not be your metaphor, but for a lot of other people, it's the thing that makes this weird, strange world click into place. It is as Gandalf instructed Frodo: "It is not our part to master all the tides of the world, but to do what is in us for the succour of those years wherein we are set, uprooting the evil in the fields that we know, so that those who live after may have clean earth to till. What weather they shall have is not ours to rule."[1]

NOTES

Introduction

1. Amanda Holpuch, "Andres Serrano's Controversial Piss Christ Goes on View in New York," *Guardian*, September 28, 2012, https://www.theguardian.com/artanddesign/2012/sep/28/andres-serrano-piss-christ-new-york.
2. Hudgins, "Piss Christ."

1. Lena Dunham Is Not a Pedophile

1. Ryan Broderick, "Lena Dunham Responds to Accusations She Sexually Abused Her Sister," BuzzFeed, November 2, 2014, https://www.buzzfeed.com/ryanhatesthis/lena-dunham-responds-to-sex-abuse-claims?utm_term=.wmbrQJ4Y0#.dxadNOV18.
2. David Walker, "Lena Dunham Is Entitled to Your Affection," *Oberlin Alumni Magazine* 109, no. 2 (Spring 2014), http://www.oberlin.edu/alummag/spring2014/lenadunham.html.
3. Fiqah, Twitter post, February 10, 2010, 10:13 p.m., http://twitter.com/sassycrass.
4. Morris, "You Don't Like the Girls in 'Girls'?"
5. Jenna Wortham, "Where (My) Girls At?" The Hairpin, April 16, 2012.
6. Reeve, "'Girls' Writer Responds to Critique of 'Girls' with Horrible Joke."
7. Bradford Thomas, "Lena Dunham Describes Sexually Abusing Her Little Sister," Truth Revolt, October 29, 2014, http://www

.truthrevolt.org/news/lena-dunham-describes-sexually-abusing
-her-toddler-sister.

2. Harry Styles Is (Probably) Not a Creep

1. Abi Buchanan, "The Real Message One Direction Is Sending to Young Girls That You Probably Didn't Think About," Thought Catalog, June 3, 2015, https://thoughtcatalog.com/abi-buchanan/2015 /06/the-real-message-one-direction-is-sending-out-to-young -girls-that-you-probably-didnt-think-about/.
2. Saper, "A Nervous Theory," 35.
3. Saper, "A Nervous Theory," 43.
4. Hammett, "The Ideological Impediment," 88.

3. On My Money and Bitches Who Better Have It

1. bell hooks, "Moving Beyond Pain," bell hooks Institute, May 9, 2016, http://www.bellhooksinstitute.com/blog/2016/5/9/moving -beyond-pain.
2. Herwees, "We R Cute Shoplifters."
3. Paul Baker, *Sexed Texts*, 166.

4. Why Does This Australian Sound Like She's from Atlanta?

1. Jeff Guo, "How Iggy Azalea Mastered Her Blaccent," *Washington Post*, January 4, 2016, https://www.washingtonpost.com/news /wonk/wp/2016/01/04/how-a-white-australian-rapper-mastered -her-blaccent/.
2. Brett Bodner, "Miley Cyrus Wishes She Could Destroy the 'Wrecking Ball' Video from 2013," *NY Daily News*, May 17, 2017, http:// www.nydailynews.com/entertainment/music/miley-cyrus-regrets -wrecking-ball-music-video-article-1.3173659.
3. Lizzy Woods, "Miley Cyrus Is the Only Feminist Icon We Need for 2016," The Tab, June 14, 2016, https://thetab.com/uk/2016/06/14 /miley-cyrus-feminist-icon-need-2016-2389.
4. Jason Lipschutz, "Taylor Swift and Nicki Minaj's Twitter Argument: A Full Timeline of the Disagreement," Billboard, July 23, 2015, http://www.billboard.com/articles/columns/pop-shop /6641794/taylor-swift-nicki-minaj-twitter-argument-timeline.

5. Tressie McMillan Cottom, "When Your Brown Body Is a White Wonderland," TressieMc, August 27, 2013, https://tressiemc.com/2013/08/27/when-your-brown-body-is-a-white-wonderland/.

5. Mother Monster and Q.U.E.E.N.

1. Click, Lee, and Holladay, "Making Monsters."
2. Womack, *Afrofuturism*.
3. Van Veen, "Vessels of Transfer."
4. English and Kim, "Now We Want Our Funk Cut," 217–30.
5. Jeff Benjamin, "Janelle Monáe Says 'Q.U.E.E.N.' is for the 'Ostracized and Marginalized,'" Fuse, September 18, 2013, http://www.fuse.tv/videos/2013/09/janelle-monae-queen-interview.
6. Click, Lee, and Holladay, "Making Monsters," 370.
7. Alyssa Rosenberg, "Janelle Monáe's Forceful Artistic Argument That Black Lives Matter," *Washington Post*, August 18, 2015, https://www.washingtonpost.com/news/act-four/wp/2015/08/18/janelle-monaes-forceful-artistic-argument-that-black-lives-matter/?utm_term=.1bace6bfabf9.
8. Janelle Monáe, Instagram post, August 12, 2015, Instagram.com/Janellemonae.

6. Friendly Fire

1. Jenny Trout, "Fat, Fandom, and 'Jessica Jones,' Or, 'Where the Fuck Were You?,'" Trout Nation, December 4, 2015, http://jennytrout.com/?p=9857.

7. Actually, It's about Ethics in Feminist Criticism

1. Jen Yamato, "Anita Sarkeesian on Life After Gamergate: I Want to be Human Again," Daily Beast, September 23, 2016, http://www.thedailybeast.com/articles/2016/09/23/anita-sarkeesian-on-life-after-gamergate-i-want-to-be-a-human-again.html.
2. Goldberg, "Feminism's Toxic Twitter Wars."
3. Ronson, *So You've Been Publicly Shamed*, 148.
4. David Smith, "Chimamanda Adichie on Transgender Row: I Have Nothing to Apologize For," *Guardian*, March 21, 2017, https://www.theguardian.com/books/2017/mar/21/chimamanda-ngozi-adichie-nothing-to-apologise-for-transgender-women.

8. Do You Even Lift, Bro?

1. Yes, that Kenneth Starr from the Bill Clinton impeachment hearings.
2. Katie Baker, "Here's the Powerful Letter the Stanford Victim Read Aloud to Her Attacker," BuzzFeed, June 3, 2016, https://www.buzzfeed.com/katiejmbaker/heres-the-powerful-letter-the-stanford-victim-read-to-her-ra?utm_term=.uxkby0nZ2#.dcVRnBOAa.
3. Kate Fagan, "So What Defines a 'Real Man' in Sports?," ESPN, November 6, 2013, http://www.espn.com/espnw/news-commentary/article/9937514/espnw-jonathan-martin-richie-incognito-incident-raises-questions-means-real-man-sports.
4. Franklin, "Enacting Masculinity," 28.
5. Franklin, "Enacting Masculinity," 30.

9. Dinos, Disasters, and Dives

1. Warner, "'Jurassic World' Star Bryce Dallas Howard Thinks Heel-gate Was Feminist."
2. Jayson Flores, "The Five Most Sexist Moments in Jurassic World," Bitch Media, July 15, 2015, https://www.bitchmedia.org/post/the-five-most-sexist-moments-in-jurassic-world.
3. Gillett, "We Shouldn't Fight for 'Gender Equality.'"

10. Selfie Game Strong

1. Ronson, *So You've Been Publicly Shamed*, 148.
2. Erin Gloria Ryan, "Selfies Aren't Empowering. They're a Cry for Help," *Jezebel*, November 12, 2013, http://jezebel.com/selfies-arent-empowering-theyre-a-cry-for-help-1468965365.
3. Beauvoir, *Second Sex*, 771–72.
4. Beauvoir, *Second Sex*, 757.
5. Vidor, dir., *Gilda*, 2000, DVD.
6. Vidor, dir., *Gilda*, 2000, DVD.

11. Pinterest Perfect

1. Devonshire, dir., *Great British Bake Off*, "Desserts," August 2014.
2. Chandler, "Why America Leads the World in Food Waste."
3. Matt Novak, "1 in 5 American Households with Children Are Food Insecure," Gizmodo, September 3, 2014, http://gizmodo

.com/1-in-5-american-households-with-children-are-food-insec
-1630119966.

4. Oh, "Trump Brags about Eating 'The Most Beautiful' Chocolate Cake," http://www.motherjones.com/politics/2017/04/trump -syria-chocolate-cake-mar-a-lago.

5. Pearlman, dir., *Chopped*, "Class Acts," 2011.

6. Johnson and Taylor, "Feminist Consumerism and Fat Activists," 945.

7. Johnson and Taylor, "Feminist Consumerism and Fat Activists," 948.

8. Thomas, dir., *John Mulaney*.

9. Doree Shafrir, "Who Benefits from the Tiny House Revolution?" BuzzFeed, July 5, 2016, https://www.buzzfeed.com/doree/who-is -the-tiny-house-revolution-for.

10. Taken from a study of winners and losers over the first seven seasons of the show, not counting special series.

11. Giada De Laurentiis et al., *Everyday Italian*.

12. Andrea Grimes, "Fuck Up the Patriarchy with This Tuna Salad," Resistance Kitchen, March 8, 2017, https://resistancekitchen .tumblr.com/post/158163284214/fuck-up-the-patriarchy-with-this -tuna-salad.

12. "I Am Often Inspired by Myself"

1. Marcotte, "Stop the Damsel in Distress Act."

2. Larson, "Amy Poehler's Confidence Lessons."

3. Daniella Diaz, "RNC Chief Critique: Clinton Didn't Smile During National Security Forum," CNN Politics, September 8, 2016, http:// www.cnn.com/2016/09/07/politics/reince-priebus-donald-trump -2016-election/.

4. Daniella Diaz. "Trump Calls Clinton 'a Nasty Woman,'" CNN Politics, October 20, 2016, http://www.cnn.com/2016/10/19/politics /donald-trump-hillary-clinton-nasty-woman/.

5. Holofcener, dir., *Parks and Recreation*, "Smallest Park."

6. Booker Smith, "Destroy the Pop Culture Think Piece," Splice Today, January 2, 2017, http://www.splicetoday.com/pop-culture /destroy-the-pop-culture-think-piece.

7. Taccone, dir., *Parks and Recreation*, "The Treaty."

8. Holland, dir., *Parks and Recreation*, "Jerry's Painting."

13. Teen Girls Are the Future and That Is a Good Thing

1. Callum Borchers, "New York Times Public Editor Says the Paper May Have Been 'Too Timid' on Trump and Russia," *Washington Post*, January 22, 2017, https://www.washingtonpost.com/news/the-fix/wp/2017/01/22/new-york-times-public-editor-says-paper-might-have-been-too-timid-on-trump-and-russia/?utm_term=.30623a377ad1.

2. Nolan D. McCaskill, "Trump Backs Bannon: The Media Is the 'Opposition Party,'" Politico, January 27, 2017, http://www.politico.com/story/2017/01/donald-trump-steve-bannon-media-opposition-party-234280.

3. Kristyle Solomon, Twitter post, December 10, 2016, 3:30 p.m., https://twitter.com/kristyleTweets/.

4. F. Quick, Twitter post, December 10, 2016, 3:40 p.m., https://twitter.com/quick13.

5. Peter Krogh, Twitter post, December 10, 2016, 3:41 p.m., https://twitter.com/shirt39/.

6. Mark Wetzler, Twitter post, December 10, 2016, 3:41 p.m., https://twitter.com/Wex2/.

7. Marc Huber, Twitter post, December 10, 2016, 3:42 p.m., https://twitter.com/UsesBadWords/.

8. Ashley Lynch. Twitter post, December 10, 2016, 3:42 p.m., https://twitter.com/ashleylynch/.

9. Mena Burke. Twitter post, December 10, 2016, 3:44 p.m., https://twitter.com/MenaBurke/.

10. Anne Helen Peterson, "Anne Hathaway Can't Win," Buzz-Feed, September 24, 2015, https://www.buzzfeed.com/annehelenpetersen/anne-hathaway-syndrome.

11. Anne Helen Peterson, "Anne Hathaway Can't Win," Buzz-Feed, September 24, 2015, https://www.buzzfeed.com/annehelenpetersen/anne-hathaway-syndrome.

12. Flynn, *Gone Girl*.

Last Notes

1. Tolkien, *Return of the King*, 854.

BIBLIOGRAPHY

Baker, Paul. *Sexed Texts: Language, Gender, and Sexuality*. London: Equinox, 2008.

Chandler, Adam. "Why America Leads the World in Food Waste." *Atlantic*, July 15, 2016.

Click, Melissa, Hyunji Lee, and Holly Wilson Holladay. "Making Monsters: Lady Gaga, Fan Identification, and Social Media." *Journal of Popular Music and Society* 36, no. 3 (2013).

de Beauvoir, Simone. *The Second Sex*. Paris: Éditions Gallimard, 1949. Reprinted with introduction by Natalie Haynes. London: Vintage/Random House, 2015.

De Laurentiis, Giada, Victoria Pearson, and Mario Batali. *Everyday Italian*. New York: Clarkson Potter, 2005.

Devonshire, Andy, dir. *The Great British Bake Off*. Series 5, episode 4, "Desserts." Aired August 2014, on BBC Two.

English, Daylanne K., and Alvin Kim. "Now We Want Our Funk Cut: Janelle Monáe's Neo-Afrofuturism." *American Studies* 52, no. 4 (2013): 217–30.

Flynn, Gillian. *Gone Girl*. New York: Broadway Books, 2012.

Franklin, Karen. "Enacting Masculinity: Antigay Violence and Group Rape as Participatory Theater." *Sexuality Research and Public Policy* 1, no. 2 (2004).

Gillett, George. "We Shouldn't Fight For Gender Equality. We Should Abolish Gender." *New Statesman*, October 2, 2014. http://www.newstatesman.com/society/2014/10/we-shouldn-t-fight-gender-equality-we-should-fight-abolish-gender.

Goldberg, Michelle. "Feminism's Toxic Twitter Wars." *Nation*, January 29, 2014. https://www.thenation.com/article/feminisms-toxic
-twitter-wars/.

Hammett, Jennifer. "The Ideological Impediment: Feminism and Film Theory." *Cinema Journal* 36, no. 2 (Winter 1997).

Herwees, Tasbeeh. "We R Cute Shoplifters." *Good*, June 1, 2016. https://www.good.is/features/issue-37-we-r-cute-shoplifters.

Holland, Dean, dir. *Parks and Recreation*. Season 3, episode 11, "Jerry's Painting." Written by Norm Hiscock. Aired April 28, 2011, on NBC.

Holofcener, Nicole, dir. *Parks and Recreation*. Season 4, episode 8, "Smallest Park." Written by Chelsea Peretti. Aired November 17, 2011, on NBC.

Hudgins, Andrew. "Piss Christ." *Slate*, April 19, 2000. http://www
.slate.com/articles/arts/poem/2000/04/piss_christ.html.

Johnston, Josee, and Judith Taylor. "Feminist Consumerism and Fat Activists: A Comparative Study of Grassroots Activism and the Dove Real Beauty Campaign." *Signs* 33, no. 4 (2008): 945.

Larson, Sarah. "Amy Poehler's Confidence Lessons." *New Yorker*, November 20, 2014. http://www.newyorker.com/culture/sarah
-larson/amy-poehlers-confidence-lessons.

Luther, Jessica. *Unsportsmanlike Conduct: College Football and the Politics of Rape*. Brooklyn NY: Edge of Sports, 2016.

Luther, Jessica, and Kavitha A. Davidson. *How to Love Sports When They Don't Love You Back*. Austin: University of Texas Press, forthcoming.

Marcotte, Amanda. "Stop the Damsel in Distress Act." *American Prospect*, February 2, 2012. http://prospect.org/article/stop-damsel
-distress-act.

Mulvey, Laura. "Visual Pleasure and Narrative Cinema." *Screen* 16, no. 3 (October 1, 1975): 6–18.

Oh, Inae. "Trump Brags About Eating 'The Most Beautiful' Chocolate Cake During Syria Missile Strike Decision." *Mother Jones*, April 12, 2017. http://www.motherjones.com/politics/2017/04/trump-syria
-chocolate-cake-mar-a-lago.

Pearlman, Michael, dir. *Chopped*. Season 9, episode 13, "Class Acts." Aired November 22, 2011, on Food Network.

Reeve, Elspeth. "'Girls' Writer Responds to Critique of 'Girls' with Horrible Joke." *Atlantic*, April 18, 2012. https://www.theatlantic.com

/entertainment/archive/2012/04/girls-writer-responds-critique
-girls-horrible-joke/329117/.

Ronson, Jon. *So You've Been Publicly Shamed*. Picador: London, 2015.

Saper, Craig. "A Nervous Theory: The Troubling Gaze of Psychoanalysis in Media Studies." *Diacritics* 21, no. 4 (1991): 33–52.

Taccone, Jorma, dir. *Parks and Recreation*. Season 4, episode 7, "The Treaty." Written by Harris Wittels. Aired on November 10, 2011, on NBC.

Thomas, Rhys, dir. *John Mulaney: The Comeback Kid*. Netflix, November 13, 2015.

Tolkien, J.R.R. *The Return of the King*. New York: Mariner Books. 2012.

van Veen, tobias c. "Vessels of Transfer: Allegories of Afrofuturism in Jeff Mills and Janelle Monáe." *Dancecult* 5, no. 2 (2013).

Vidor, Charles, dir. *Gilda*. 1946; Los Angeles CA: Sony Motion Picture Classics, 2000. DVD.

Walker, David. "Lena Dunham Is Entitled to Your Affection." *Oberlin Alumni Magazine* 109 no. 2 (Spring 2014). http://www.oberlin.edu/alummag/spring2014/lenadunham.html.

Warner, Kara. "'Jurassic World' Star Bryce Dallas Howard Thinks Heelgate Was Feminist." *Cosmopolitan*, October 20, 2015. http://www.cosmopolitan.com/entertainment/movies/q-and-a/a47996/bryce-dallas-howard-jurassic-world-interview/.

Womack, Ytasha L. *Afrofuturism: The World of Black Sci-Fi and Fantasy Culture*. Chicago: Chicago Review Press, 2013.